Sir Charlie

Sir Charlie

EDWIN P. HOYT

ROBERT HALE · LONDON

© *Edwin P. Hoyt 1977*
First published in Great Britain 1977

ISBN 0 7091 6192 1

Robert Hale Limited,
Clerkenwell House,
Clerkenwell Green,
London EC1R 0HT

Printed in Great Britain by Lowe & Brydone Ltd., Thetford
Photoset and bound by Weatherby Woolnough, Wellingborough

Contents

Illustrations

PICTURE CREDITS

Popperfoto: 1, 6, 8, 26, 28, 29, 30
London Borough of Lambeth Archive Dept: 2
National Film Archive Stills Library: 3, 9
Radio Times Hulton Picture Library: 4, 5, 10, 11, 14, 15, 16, 17, 18, 19, 23
Paul Rotha Museum of Modern Art, New York: 7
The Roy Export Co. Establishment: 12, 13, 20, 22
Columbia Pictures: 2
Camera Press: 24, 25, 27, 31

Preface

What possible reason could there be for a new book about Charlie Chaplin? Thousands of newspaper articles, hundreds of magazine articles, scores of books, have been devoted to this genius of the film art whose stormy career spanned three vital burgeoning decades in America. Chaplin has been analyzed, dissected, praised, lampooned and damned for his art and for his life, and sometimes for both together, particularly when the damning became almost endemic in America in the 1940s and 1950s.

But that is precisely the reason for my interest in a new book on Chaplin in the 1970s, in the twilight of his life, when passion has been spent—both his own and that of the cousins of his adopted country. Somehow something happened between Charles Chaplin and America that has never been properly explained or thoroughly resolved. What happened, when did it happen, and why did it happen?

Those are the questions that led me to undertake this book; for I belong to a generation of Americans that is deeply stained by the guilt of our fathers and elders in the post-war years of the 1940s and 1950s. The depth of that guilt in relation to our own dissidents in unravelling in the 1970s through such studies as E. J. Kahn's work on the 'China hands' who were disgraced and driven from American government service in the McCarthy years—all quite wrongly as history has shown.

Chaplin was as much a victim of these times as John Davies, John Service and Charles W. Thayer, all dedicated American public servants who happened to be right at a time when being right was no excuse. These men were driven into exile, and so was Chaplin, for in the second decade of the twentieth century he had cast his lot with America, no matter what passport he carried. Beverly Hills was his home, Hollywood was his milieu, and Americans comprised his biggest market and, for more than a decade, his strongest supporters and his greatest admirers.

How it changed! The burden of this book is in the manner of that change, as well as the manner of development of Charles Chaplin, the film genius. In a way one followed the other, for in the beginning a young Chaplin came to a young country and entered a young industry. They grew together, industry, performer and audience, and in the years of the great European War of 1914-18 and the early 1920s, Chaplin could do little wrong. England treated him with less honour and respect in this period than did America; it seemed natural enough in London that England should expect this son to come home and fight for his country. From Beverly Hills the view was quite different, and from on high the futility of the argument is apparent, for the undersized Chaplin could scarcely have contributed much to the British war effort as a soldier, whereas in *Shoulder Arms* alone he contributed much of that genius, to say nothing of all the other films he made to titillate and delight audiences in the war-weary world.

The French, as disinterested parties, discovered Charlot —the little fellow—in the war years, and their view has a certain validity because of the disinterest. The French have never slackened in their enthusiasm for Chaplin and his work, for neither the political excitement that seized America, the puritanism that affected the same country, nor the feeling of *lèse majesté* that troubled Britain were duplicated in France. Most Americans could not seem to understand that Chaplin was an artistic anarchist who refused to be bound by normal political or social convention. Britons were annoyed by his flagrant lack of patriotic virtue and by what they saw as disrespect for royalty and English convention when Chaplin disregarded a royal summons during his second European trip. The French simply did not care about such immaterialities; in no way did these attitudes penetrate the Gallic soul. And of course from a world view, this same unconsciousness of wrongdoing prevailed; the offences Chaplin committed in America were totally offences against Anglo-Saxon *mores*.

Looking at Chaplin's problems from a slightly different view, examine his reception by the Russians. He came into his own in Russia in the 1920s. The Russians loved the little clown of the early pictures. When he produced *Modern Times* the Soviets were confused by the factory scenes and the social commentary. They loved *The Great Dictator*—but only after Hitler marched into Russia, breaching the Berlin-Moscow alliance. They hated *Monsieur Verdoux,* but in the final analysis they revered the little clown whose antics pleased a whole world. Unlike the French, and certain Anglo-Saxon intellectuals, they never cared much for Chaplin's later work. That work beginning with *A Woman of Paris* in 1923, represented the mature Chaplin, who had a social message to deliver. France saw the maturing, recognized the process, and French critics associated the comic and the tragic in the manner that Chaplin seems to have intended. I say seems, because from time to time Chaplin has reverted to the claim that all he ever wanted to do in the world was to be funny —when his feature films have gone much further than that. Indeed, *Limelight,* which is a particularly British celebration of Chaplin's life and beliefs, was called by critic Gavin Lambert "a deep, calm fatal emanation of sadness".

I belong to a generation that first encountered Chaplin in these mature years. I recall seeing *City Lights* as a child when it was released as a feature film, but for some reason that film did not move me much. I recall with a much greater sense of excitement and satisfaction *Modern Times,* which was shown in the midst of the Great American Depression, and which I understood very generally. I believe I missed such matters as the 'significance' of the scene where Chaplin picked up a red flag that had fallen from the back of a truck, and was immediately swept into a revolutionary demonstration. That was a highly controversial scene and led to Chaplin's castigation as a red-hot radical, but I was then as innocent as Chaplin and merely thought it funny. When I saw *The Great Dictator* my reaction as a youth to the six-minute soliloquy at the end of the film was largely boredom. Chaplin was pleading for the Christian ethic—I went to Sunday school and was more willing to accept the idea from our Episcopal minister. The little Jewish barber was pathetic, the dictator Hynkel was ridiculous, Jack Oakie as Dictator Napaloni was hilarious, and Paulette Goddard as the girl was gorgeous and stirring to a callow youth of the 1940s.

Politically, in these years I was not very profound or even very interested. Chaplin's pronouncements about the need for a second front came at a time when I was involved in my own 'second front' in Assam and Burma, and over there most of us who read the capsulized versions of *Time* and *Newsweek* wondered at all the excitement. We were getting on with our war, not very well, but actively. We were as puzzled as the next man about the strange alliance with Russia. In effect we were being told that the Russians were our friends, but there was a suspicion that those who told us had their fingers crossed behind their backs. Of course all this came out in 1946, when the Russians and Americans locked horns along their mutual frontiers, from Germany to Korea. I happened to be in Korea and shared the general irritation of the American high command with the Russian intransigence on matters we saw with crystal clarity: all that had to be done was let a native Korean government unify the country. In our own way we were as simplistic as Chaplin in these days; he was defending the right of the Russians to protect themselves with border bastions.

I returned to America in 1947 for a visit. That was the year of *Monsieur Verdoux*. I believe I actually saw the film in Paris much later in the year. I found it amusing, but puzzling. Again the simplicity of Chaplin's cry puzzled and evaded me: a man who murders a few is a murderer; the governors and industrialists who set up wars are heroes.

I felt then that the message got in the way of the humour. Of course the French took it quite differently, theirs was a level of sophistication that appreciated simplicity for its own sake. A naïve American could understand the Christian ethic, but wondered what earthly good could come from presenting it in a motion-picture theatre.

I returned to America in the last year of the 1940s, and was quite shocked at the miasma that seemed to have settled over my country. I can recall quite clearly encountering an

old friend from post-war days in China, who was literally in
fear for his job on a Luce publication because, like so many
of us, he had been open in his criticism of the Chinese
Nationalists and loud in our shared prognostication that the
Communists would, and should win the revolutionary
struggle. We were so naïve as to believe the Communists
would improve the lot of the Chinese people, and that this
was adequate reason for them to come to power. We simply
did not conceive that our America would have a vested
interest in the maintenance of the imperial and oppressive
status quo in many countries. In reviewing Charles Chaplin's
life, I see the naïvety of my own.

By 1949 the dreadful air of purge and intimidation had
settled over America. It was not entirely political. I recall the
hysteria that shook all America when film actress Ingrid
Bergman announced from Italy that she was forsaking her
doctor husband and her children and going to live in sin
with Italian film director Roberto Rossellini. Miss Bergman
had been a particular favourite with Americans, in a manner
reminiscent of Charles Chaplin in a way. She represented
cleanliness and wholesomeness in most of the rôles she
played: nun, happy housewife, brave woman in war. For her
to cast caution and her image into the winds thus was a
grave affront to the puritanism endemic in America, and
aroused righteous fury in this period of unhappiness and
confusion when the world was not turning out at all as Mr
Roosevelt and Mr Churchill had forecast in their brave
wartime speeches. The Press and public turned on Miss
Bergman with a viciousness reminiscent of what had happened to Charles Chaplin in the 1920s with his divorces, and
in the 1940s with his paternity suit and a trial on federal
morals charges.

In this same atmosphere, many Hollywood personalities
were brought into the spotlight of the political hysteria
created and nourished in the infighting between Republicans
and Democrats in Washington. It manifested itself in
Senator McCarthy's wholesale charges against the federal
government establishment for being "soft on communism".
It was fed by some specific incidents of treason and espionage
that were definitely traceable to the Soviet Union. The Hiss

case, the Rosenberg case, and half a dozen others were real. In this atmosphere Congressional committees began rooting in Hollywood for communists, and in their efforts uncovered some communist adherents, and a number of troubled idealists. Chaplin did not much differentiate; he had friends who were far to the left, and he had friends who were idealists, and some who were as naïve as he was. He tried to protect them. He spoke for them, and he earned the enmity of all the red-haters and red-baiters in America because he was rich, and wealth meant power.

And so all the old charges of the past were raked up. Chaplin became an enemy of the people once again; this time the combination of moral purism and political purism grated roughly on him. He and his fourth wife, Oona, were raising a family, and they wondered if the poisonous atmosphere that surrounded them was healthy for the children.

The question was brought to a head in the most ignoble way that a government could behave toward an individual. Chaplin and his family went abroad on a trip, and he was given assurances before he left that all was well in his official relations with America. But he had scarcely sailed from the American shore than the government dishonoured its promise to him, and then government, Press, and much of the public covered the dreadful act by assuming a holy attitude. Having hurt Chaplin, his enemies hated him all the more.

This, then, was the final ignoble act for which Americans had real need to be ashamed. They had, in ejecting this artistic genius because of his ideas, shown how little reality there was in the 1950s in the celebrated patriotic song that speaks of the "land of the free and the home of the brave". The barring of Charles Chaplin from American shores was neither an act of freedom nor a celebration of bravery.

Chaplin's bitterness caused him then to refer to the "iron curtain" with which America had surrounded itself, and there was enough truth in the statement to give thoughtful Americans pause and cause them shame for the intolerance of a nation that supposedly revered that virtue.

A handful of people stood up for Chaplin, but their voices were drowned out in the cacophony of hysterical screaming, led by many of the same elements of the Press and politics that had been loudest in their condemnation of the Bergman-Rossellini affair. This unhappy state of affairs continued through the 1950s and into the 1960s. By the end of that decade, a certain numb realization began to come to America: the basic assumption that the world could be divided into right and wrong, free and slave, was not proving out. Americans, the self-styled leaders of the freedom bloc, were allied with enslavers the world over, and in South-east Asia were actually engaged in the process of wholesale killing for political reasons. American leaders still talked in the old phrases—freedom, life, liberty; but many in the world had long since stopped believing, and in this decade so did many Americans.

It was then that America began to see the actual world more clearly than at any time since the end of World War II. And it was in this period of reappraisal and awakening that America made its peace with Charles Chaplin. It was late, but it was not too late.

Indeed, as I review the proofs of this book in the winter of 1977, there seems a new air sweeping across America. It is not just the change in administrations—although this is a part of it—nor is it a basic change in the world scene. Perhaps it is a leavening, a happy combination of time and changed ambitions. England, having come through a dreadful period of inflation, uncertainty, and negativism, seems again to savour the sound of a bird singing. In America there is not the meadowlark to cheer us, but we have, besides the eagle and the mocking bird, the clear, sweet call of the dove.

Edwin P. Hoyt
Honolulu, 1977

1

Sir Charlie

On 1st January, 1975, Mr Charles Chaplin was knighted by the Queen. In a public sense that honour was a happy ending to one of the great human stories of our era; Charles Chaplin's "indomitable little man beset with adversity", as *The Times* called him, was the real Charles Chaplin, citizen of the world, and the representative of all of us. In a private sense, Mr Chaplin's acceptance of the honour after several refusals, indicated his own final arrival at a contentment he had long deserved, and which had been withheld from him in recent years by forces over which neither he nor his critics had any control.

Too often genius leaves the world unhappily. A few men, like George Bernard Shaw, become 'institutions' or legends early, and remain that way. Some, like Sir Winston Churchill, rise to the heights, to be cast into the depths, and to rise again even higher. The story of Sir Charles is more like that of Churchill than of Shaw in several ways; most important because Chaplin, like Churchill, was brought down by politics and not primarily by failure in his art. And yet even here there are anomalies; Chaplin's art-form changed under him in the middle of his career, and that change, coupled with his own maturity as a human being, hastened the disaster that came to him. Sir Charlie was lucky to find a neutral haven where he was safe from his enemies and his former friends. He was luckier to live long enough to see the world change so that a point of view that had once been an anathema in Britain and even more so in the United States was made innocent by events. The Charles Chaplin of the 1940s and 1950s was regarded as a flaming radical. The views he held can be assumed to be unchanged; in the 1970s they would not alone secure him an airing on an American college campus or in an English public meeting. All along, Chaplin was espousing essentially Christian philosophical ideas. But aside from that, a world overwhelmed by terror and nihilism must regard the espousal of the rights of the common man as beside the point. Sitting in the sunshine of his life in his Swiss villa, surrounded by a loving family, Sir Charles seems to have overcome the bitterness forced upon him and come to terms with a world that once more shows signs of being ready for his comedy.

For years that comedy has been respected by a minor segment of enthusiasts, historians and collectors in the West. But in the 1970s Chaplin revivals were cropping up around the world, and in the winter of 1975-76 television stations in America were undertaking series of Chaplin short films, to run week after week. It is a far cry from the old days of the silent films, when Chaplin's movies outdrew nearly all others; it is too much to expect generations that have grown up on videotape and the wide colour screen to accept uncritically the physical limitations of the early cinema processes. Probably the physical limitations will always stand between Charlot, the little man, and a revival of the mass acceptance that marked his early career. The world moves on, the clock does not turn back, but Sir Charles Chaplin's life deserves more critical analysis that it has received, or than was possible to give it before he published *My Auto-biography* a dozen years ago. His more recent *My Life in Pictures* is essentially a recapitulation of his film art. But what Sir Charles chose to discuss and what he chose not to discuss in the autobiography is more telling. The world is still interested in the entertainments of Charles Chaplin. The world can see much of interest about itself in the mirror of Chaplin's life and the ways in which he was warped by events.

Chaplin's biographers had no way of knowing, until *My Autobiography,* just how deeply was the seat of all Chaplin's life embedded in one of the most wretched childhoods out-side the pages of Dickens. Of course that general comparison could be made of anyone, and the world of Freud and Jung would find it obvious. But the saying and the detail are two different matters. The first hundred pages of *My Autobiography* reveal far more about the adult Chaplin and the Charlie character than most self-told tales. They also show very simply just why Charles Chaplin became the kind of political creature he did when war forced him to adopt a political stance for the first time in his life.

For example, when Chaplin became immensely successful in America and had no further economic worries, it was a source of wonder to many that he was extremely careful of money. Such an attitude was out of tune with the others of his milieu. Read *My Autobiography* and it is simple enough to see reason: once there was a sea captain from Nantucket who was shipwrecked and nearly starved for weeks. He was rescued and survived, and many years later when he died, his Nantucket house was found stuffed with food, even in the attics and crannies. The almost unremitting poverty of the young Chaplin obviously created in him a very careful approach to money. He never lived as opulently as Fatty Arbuckle or Harold Lloyd or others of his peers. Of course he would become a saver. At the crisis of his life, his habit of keeping large liquid assets saved him from difficulty with an America that had turned against him. In the autobiography, one can sense the fear that assailed Chaplin when he and his money were parted after he left America in 1952.

The poverty, then, was a part of the Chaplin luck. He had the acquisitiveness of a merchant. It was a childhood trait and the poverty was not entirely responsible for it; he said himself that he was always as a boy occupied with various business schemes, from selling flowers in pubs (wearing a black crêpe arm-band) to blowing glass—an occupation that lasted one whole day. These jobs, as a doctor's boy, page, toymaker, second-hand clothing dealer, would all show their tracks in his art as time went on. Once he was given a job feeding a huge printing press; some of the terror of machinery this engendered would show itself in the factory sequences of *Modern Times*.

Illness, insanity, and institutions played large rôles in the young Chaplin's life. Throughout his later work one can sense a general distrust of a social system that permitted such poverty and depersonalization of the human being. Chaplin's

East End and Lambeth are scarcely recognizable today physically, so much have they changed that most of his old landmarks of the 1890s have disappeared. But more than the physical change has been the social and economic difference that has come about in three-quarters of a century. The real world of hunger and rags and fear that Chaplin conjures from his youth is no more; it is well gone in a London that has heeded 'the little fellow's' cries from the depths in the 1920s and 1930s.

Then there is the question of Chaplin's America. As it has done with so many others, America has tried to assimilate Chaplin, and when he proved himself unassailably British, to chew up and spit him out. Lest chauvinists take heart, Britons in this same era of the 1940s and 1950s showed too little forbearance to make them proud. A Shavian iconoclast or a hermit lord might arouse British admiration; a fiercely independent Chaplin who snubbed an indirect royal summons brought an adder's response. And there were many who assailed Charles Chaplin's politics with a resentment they did not even show Sir Oswald Mosley at the height of his aberrations. It was a shame, particularly since the world later learned that Chaplin's politics represented innocence, not conspiracy. Still, it was America that forced Chaplin to his own excesses, and then treated him as dishonestly as ever an artist has been treated anywhere. A handful of hysterical politicians in half a decade managed to destroy dozens of valuable careers; it is possible that Charles Chaplin was lucky to leave America when he did; otherwise he might have been badgered by the authorities into a prison term. It is an American tradition to demand that its heroes conform to the *mores* of the moment, and it is apparent from Chaplin's subsequent work that he could never do just that. There is an element of the ridiculous here: Chaplin had tremendous difficulties with the film industry's self-censorship committees; twenty years later the concept of film censorship in America had apparently vanished totally. It will return, and someday in the American emotional cycle will probably be as repressive and ridiculous as it was in the 1940s and 1950s.

One aspect of the Chaplin story that makes it ever new is the comedy. Forever Chaplin's name is invoked by the students and practitioners of the art. In the summer of 1975, in London, the celebrated mime Marcel Marceau gave fulsome praise to Chaplin as a source of his own art. So the comedy of Charles Chaplin lives on and will live on, because of its simple treatment of universal themes. Millions of words, hundreds of articles, scores of books, have been devoted to the art of Charlie Chaplin. In recent years the French have seemed most interested; perhaps that is because Chaplin retired to French-speaking Switzerland. But in all countries, in nearly all languages, that art has been assessed and will continue to be. The change is the most interesting aspect of Chaplin's art, change from the early stage buffoon and silent-picture clown to the erudite spokesman that is Chaplin in the morality study *Monsieur Verdoux*. Here Chaplin seems to have reached the apex of his social development. *Limelight* was offered at the hour of Chaplin's crisis, so for years it laboured under the political stigma, and was boycotted in America as a part of that particular national tantrum. As for *A King in New York*, Chaplin himself had nothing to say in his autobiography, and when he was interviewed in Switzerland by writer Harold Clurman, the subject was tacitly left out of the discussions. *A King in New York* might be called 'Charlie's revenge'; it was a bittersweet comedy that delved into America and its institutions. But Charles Chaplin was too close to the source, and too much involved, to be able to treat adequately of America. There was none of the simple greatness of *The Great Dictator* here. By Chaplin's own obvious admission, the film was a failure.

It is a sad finale to a great artistic career, yet the fact remains that nothing Chaplin could do in these latter years would diminish the artistry of the past. It is equally true that the 'message' films produced after 1936 will always have a more select audience than the body of Chaplin's work. In the beginning, and in the middle, he was the great clown of the world. In his own maturity he felt the need to use his art to express emotions and beliefs, not just to make people laugh. The issues fade into nothingness. The television series *Startrek* is interesting if for no other reason than that it gives us a preview of the reason for the fading of history; but the little man with the baggy pants and the odd moustache will be funny forever.

Another aspect of Chaplin's life that has bemused at least the American public has been his sex life. As scores of articles in dozens of Hollywood publications have indicated, it was certainly an active and varied life. When Chaplin was writing his autobiography, a lady writer asked if he had the courage to tell 'the truth' and she meant the truth about his amours. She must have been an American, for that is the kind of question that would bother a female American novelist. Chaplin does not record his retort, but his reply is contained in the autobiography. He deals with women, with love, and to a certain extent with sex. Women certainly played an important rôle in all of Charles Chaplin's life. The very humanity that made him so great a clown also made him extremely susceptible to women. He tells one tale of an unrequited love when he was nearly in his twentieth year that does much to explain his marriages to Mildred Harris, Lita Grey, and Oona O'Neill, and the attraction that very young women had for him.

It seems likely that Charles Chaplin would have made a success of anything to which he turned his hand. Throughout life he exhibited the drive and determination that breeds good luck; in 1914 alone he made thirty-five motion pictures. To be sure, most of these were one-reel films, but the young Chaplin was obviously working very hard. As he and the medium matured, the Chaplin films became longer and more complex, until in 1923 he tried his first full-length feature, *A Woman of Paris*.

The career really began in 1901. Before that time he had appeared on the stage intermittently since he was five years old, but when he was twelve he secured a part through the Blackmore Agency in the Strand, and £2 10s. a week in a play called *Jim*, went on tour, and soon had another job in a vaudeville sketch, earning £3 a week. After a few ups and downs he was hired by the impresario Fred Karno, and then it was up, up, up. By the time Chaplin was nineteen he was a successful comedian in London, he and his brother had a comfortable flat in Brixton Road and the next year he went to Paris. Soon enough he was in New York for Karno, and then on the road in America, making $75 a week and banking two-thirds of it. On his second tour of America he was signed by the film-maker Mack Sennett for twice as much money. Before he was twenty-five he was directing his own comedies for Sennett at $200 a week. The next jump was a big one, to Essanay films, for $12,000 a week and a $10,000 bonus. Then it was $10,000 for each picture.

Chaplin was such a success in the years of World War I that he could not travel across America by train without having fans mob him at the stopping points along the way. Mutual films gave him a $670,000 contract, one of the largest ever given anyone in the industry in those years. Chaplin was already a phenomenon.

Unlike many geniuses, however, he had a sharp sense of double-entry bookkeeping. Others might be exploited by the film makers, but not Chaplin. The money was in making films, so he would make them and write them and cast them and direct them and play in them. He did this for Mutual. He did it for more money for First National. As the war ended, he joined with such luminaries as Mary Pickford and Douglas Fairbanks to form United Artists on the principle that the artists should profit from their own efforts. The success, going into the millions of dollars, was so pronounced that Charles Chaplin built his own studio. In the 1920s he was firmly linked with America and the American system; the Japanese Black Dragon Society called him "the darling of the capitalist class" and considered murdering him when he visited Japan in order to create an incident with the United States. From then on Chaplin never looked back, in terms of success and acceptance, until the political years began. There was trouble with *The Great Dictator* which created rumblings in South America. It was quieted by the realities of the war, yet there are indications that here Chaplin had aroused politicians to his effectiveness as a spokesman for 'the little people'. Seven years later, when *Monsieur Verdoux* was completed, Chaplin had been politicized by events and the blind hatred of pressure groups.

One might ask what brought about this politicization? Chaplin's life tells us: he educated himself, beginning with Dickens in the London days, going on to philosophy and economics. And more than books, he was educated by coming into personal contact with nearly any and all of the world's great that he might wish to see, and many who sought him out after the 1920s because of his international reputation. International—that was the point. It was this very internationalism that brought Chaplin finally to his crisis and breach with America. In the changing years of the 1940s the Americans found themselves as the basic force of one international political bloc, and as a critic Chaplin suffered for his international outlook and his refusal to become an American citizen. He had come to these positions gradually, after much travel around the world. He had a message, and he felt the need to use the talking picture to add a dimension to his pantomime. Thus did his art change in the politicization of the artist.

From this came a kind of purgatory in which Chaplin did not feel at home, either in his native Britain or his adopted America. He sought refuge in the blandest country of Europe, but again a land that is noted for its internationalism. There was something quite fitting in placing Charlot, the 'little fellow' here, with equal access, by Swiss custom, to all the political philosophies of the world.

In his autobiography, Sir Charles indicated that he had given the world its last Chaplin picture. He would write, perhaps, and direct perhaps, and otherwise shepherd the work of others but his own work was done; *A King in New York* of 1957 was the end of it.

A score of years later, then, with most of the residues of hysteria wiped from the corners of the western world in which he lived and worked, perhaps there is something to be added to the understanding of this artist and the way in which he was beneficiary, victim and contributor to the history of his times.

2

Sweet and Sour Youth

If you are going to understand the mature Charles Chaplin any better than did his own generation, you are going to have to begin with his mother, and with some scenes of one of the most dismal childhoods to exist outside the pages of fiction. The miserable youth of this little Londoner is as complete an explanation as any human being needs of the reason for Britain's welfare state that came into being half a century later.

Charles was born on 16 April 1889, in the district of Walworth but soon moved to Lambeth, around which his life would be loosely centred for the next dozen years. He was named after his father: Charles Spencer Chaplin, who was a popular baritone on the music-hall circuit in the last vigorous days of the Victorian era. His mother, Hannah, was also a performer, then a handsome woman in her twenties who sang and danced with various companies including the D'Oyly Carte. The family background was Jewish, French, Spanish, Irish and gypsy. Charles' half-brother Sidney, was four years older, the son of Hannah and a Jewish bookmaker. This mixture of backgrounds and races, plus the great levellers of theatrical background and poverty, contributed one great attribute to the life of the boy that would persist in the man. He was totally devoid of social prejudice. He always would be. His great social hatred was reserved for poverty. As one of his biographers, Robert Payne, put it, the very word aroused in Chaplin a "kind of growling horror that the thing should exist".

His own poverty was the result of drink, and there, too, lay an explanation of character. In his adult life Chaplin was general abstemious. He rarely drank to excess, and his atti-

tude about those many talented people around him who did
so, such as John Barrymore, alternated between rage and
pity. In drunkenness Chaplin could see only too well his own
father, whose career and life were eventually destroyed by
drink.

The first few years of Chaplin's life seemed secure enough.
As with many brilliant people, his conscious memory began
early. He could recall events of his fourth year clearly. The
family lived in comfortable rooms then and they had the
means to keep a housemaid. He recalled the gaiety of a
London spring, of his mother as a prospering actress, and of
rounds of entertainments.

Chaplin's was a most 'liberal' family in the political and
social senses. In later life in Puritan America of the 1920s, the
seeds of Chaplin's destruction would first be sowed in a
moral sense. The America that turned irrevocably against the
ingenious comedian Fatty Arbuckle would also begin to turn
on that greater folk her 'Charlie' over moral issues he could
never quite understand. His mother had run away from
home when she was sixteen years old, and she had married
three times. In the days of her youth 'actress' was a synonym
for 'fallen woman'. Coming from such a background no one
could expect Charles Chaplin to share a Victorian sense of
morality let alone an American hatred for the obvious.

The breakdown of secure life began when Charles was five
years old. His mother was successful enough then, but her
health was giving out, and her voice began to fail. One night,
while playing at the Aldershot Canteen, it failed entirely,
and she could not go on. Little Charlie was with her that
night, and the stage manager recalled that the boy had a
little act of his own; he could sing popular songs with some
grace. Charlie was shoved out onto the stage, sang the coster
song *Jack Jones,* and brought down the house in cheers and
laughter. Coppers and even bits of silver began to pour on to
the stage. Showing a neat sense of finance that would never
leave him, the boy artist stopped his singing, and told the
audience that he would pick up the money and then continue his act. That announcement brought more laughter,
and the stage manager, who came with a handkerchief to
help Charlie, picked up the money. Again, exhibiting

ingrained suspicion of officialdom that would never leave him, Charlie suspected that the stage manager was going to keep the money, and so confided in normal tones to the audience.

This was as funny as a stand-up comedy act, and the audience howled as the manager made off stage with the money with the urchin anxiously following.

As Chaplin recalled in his autobiography, his mother was in the wings to take the money, and the relieved performer then returned to the stage. Another song—more cheers, more money—and when his mother came to carry him off, a tremendous burst of applause for the most spontaneous entertainment the Aldershot Canteen had seen in many a moon.

Hannah Chaplin's theatrical career ended sharply that year, and she had never been of a saving nature, so their world began to collapse around them. They moved from their three comfortable rooms, and soon were down to one room in grubby surroundings. Hannah took to religion and carried the little Charles with her in body, but not in spirit. The church to him would always be trappings and long sermons; whatever religion the adult Chaplin would have would be an extremely private matter.

Chaplin's own phrase for the next few years of his boyhood is "cheerless twilight". They lived the wretched existence of London's poor. Sometimes his mother got an odd job, nursing for one, dressmaking for another. At this same time drink began to do for Chaplin's father, and his support became sporadic. Supposedly he contributed ten shillings a week to his estranged wife and the two boys; actually weeks went by when there was no money coming from him at all.

Little by little Hannah Chaplin sold her worldly goods, as they moved from place to place. In his adult years Chaplin was to anchor himself in a single house in Beverly Hills that would survive three and a half marriages, and he would only be driven away from it by the power of the United States government. No one need wonder whence came Chaplin's intense sense of place and possessions. He could recall poignantly his mother's marvellous theatrical trunk, from which she could extract a judge's wig or a soubrette's spangles.

Piece by piece it all went to the pawnbroker or was sold.

Religion and recollection were Hannah Chaplin's diversions from the grim reality of sooty lower-class London. Charles was her almost constant companion and she read to him from the Bible and spoke to him of the theatre. The latter became the one connecting link that persisted in these wretched years.

Hannah lived from day to day, unable to contemplate the future. When Sidney found a heavy purse, she spent the money on new clothes for the boys and took them to the seashore on holiday. For Chaplin it was an unforgettable experience, but it was also disastrous. Soon their financial plight became so desperate that the vendors repossessed her sewing machine and cut off Hannah's main source of income. Chaplin's father had succumbed completely to drink; he did not work at all and could not make the ten-shilling payments. He went to the hospital. His wife and the children went to the Lambeth workhouse. It was another lovely summer, June 1896.

The enormity of the change struck the little boy only when they had actually entered the dismal institutional gates, and then the portals of the building. In the lobby, they were met by authority, and there with no warning, the boys were sent in one direction and their mother in another. The shock was tremendous. There was no recollection of budding trees or singing birds that day, as there had been on other momentous occasions in the spring.

Soon, the boys were transferred to Hanwell Schools for Orphans and Destitute Children, a few miles outside London. Life was irrepressible, the adult Chaplin could recall the beauty of the trip through the green English spring countryside. The joy was short lived, however, for at their destination the boys were separated and Charlie at seven was put in with the young ones, while eleven-year-old Sidney went with the older boys.

It was a Dickensian atmosphere: drab uniforms, shaved heads, thin soups and gruels and the flat food of the institution, the rod and the birch; all the dreadful impersonality of an uncaring society. In his autobiography, Chaplin devotes eight pages to the seven dreary months he spent at

Hanwell and recalls all the depressing detail. Sydney escaped
first, in November of that year, 1896, to the naval training
ship *Exmouth,* when he reached the age of twelve. Charles was
scheduled to remain four more years, but Hannah Chaplin
managed to get out of the workhouse and find some promise
of employment. In January she retrieved Charles, and soon
Sydney came home from the training ship as well.

The joy of reconciliation was brief. It was the same old
tale: mother sick, father drunk and unable to work, and back
to the state institution, this time at Norwood. Soon a new
disaster, their mother had collapsed and become irrational
and was confined to the Cane Hill insane asylum.

Dispassionate justice brought the boys out of the institution and decreed that they should be supported by their
father. He had taken up lodgings in the Kennington Road
with a ladylove, and this was to be their new home. Charles
fared well enough there for a time, for the lady took a liking
to him, but she took a violent dislike to Sydney. His life was
most unpleasant. But so then did Charles begin to share in
it, for their father's dissolution was increasing apace, and he
spent less and less time at home, more in the pubs. One night
the eight-year-old Charles came to the house to find it empty
and when no one appeared for hours, he went out into the
streets, roaming until past midnight, and then coming to sit
on the kerb and wait. On another night he and Sydney were
found at three o'clock in the morning sleeping beside a
watchman's fire near the house.

Authority again entered their life in the form of the
Society for Prevention of Cruelty to Children, and somehow
their mother was released from the asylum, and the family
came together again, to live off Kennington Road between a
pickle factory and a slaughterhouse.

Charlie went to school. He had gone before, at Hanwell
and Norwood, but the spells of education were so variegated
that his interest was captured only by theatrics. At Hanwell
his teacher would remember him in later years as a little
clown who amused the other children by antics and
grimaces. At the school near the pickle factory he achieved
a certain fame, but again through theatrics not scholarship.
His mother had taught him a comedy recitation entitled

Miss Priscilla's Cat, and when he had memorized it Charles recited it one day for some of the boys. His teacher heard, and thought the performance so amusing that he eventually recited before every classroom in the school. The triumph gave him a taste of glory.

Hard economics, however, brought Charles Chaplin into the theatrical life that would consume him and raise him to a pinnacle in a very few years. His father knew the manager of The Eight Lancashire Lads, a troupe of seven boys and a girl with a bowl haircut, who toured the counties with a clog-dance routine. Charles would have his keep with the troupe, and his mother would have a half a crown a week. The boy would become an asset instead of a liability.

Charles was an inventive boy, and he dreamed of acts of his own, as they toured here and there, going to a different school each week as the act moved. When the company was signed for appearance on the vaudeville bill at London's Palladium, Charles had his first independent part: he was chosen to do a comedy sketch with the famous French clown Marceline. The bit called for him to play the part of a cat more or less as a prop for the clown. Soon, Charles was making improvisations, and stealing scenes from the principal. The real Charlie Chaplin was born.

The child performer was lucky to see many an actor, the famous of London's music-hall stage. He watched Marie Lloyd and learned from her. He saw Bransby Williams, the Dickens player and became so enthralled with Williams' portrayal of various characters, that he bought a copy of *Oliver Twist.* It was his first educational purchase, and signalled an interest in books that would eventually give Chaplin the education his style of life denied him as a boy.

With Dickens and Williams as his guides, young Charles tried to develop an act of his own, imitating the imitator. His mentor, the head of the clog troupe, thought he did very well, but when the act was tried on an audience, it was a dismal failure, and so Charles took up acrobatics, until he fell in an act one day. Then he turned to comedy juggling, and practised endlessly in his room with rubber balls and tin plates.

After a few months the clog dancers were disbanded, and

Charles went back to London to live with his mother in a miserable garret at 3 Pownall Terrace. This place became the centre of Charles' existence for some time.

Life offered the same misery and no more than they had before the clog-dancing interlude. Charles' father was now dying of his alcoholism, in St Thomas's Hospital on the Albert Embankment. There could be no more help from that source. Sydney had a job as a telegraph boy, but they were so poor that Sydney's one decent suit of clothes had to be pawned during the week, while Hannah Chaplin earned the seven shillings to redeem it out for the weekend, then repawned it on Monday as Sydney donned his uniform. Charles wore his Eight Lancashire Lads' costume until it was literally in rags. When the senior Chaplin died, he would have been buried in a pauper's grave, except for the intervention of an uncle from Africa, who paid the funeral expenses.

The death of his father brought Charles Chaplin to his first business venture: flower vending in pubs when he wore a black armband and elicited sympathy, until his mother forbade him to earn his money even indirectly through an establishment that served drink.

He had many little jobs. He was chandler's boy and doctor's boy, page boy, errand boy, and when he was about ten years old he had the frightening experience with the big printing press, a job which lasted three weeks before he came down with influenza.

Several biographers indicated that in this period Charles spent two years at the Hern Boys College near London, but Chaplin does not mention the place in his autobiography. Instead, he speaks of various ups and downs, all centring around that miserable garret in Pownall Terrace. There were times when they made ends meet, through Hannah's sewing and Sydney's efforts. Sydney got a job as a bugler on a passenger boat on the Africa run. He also waited at tables in second-class and earned a fair amount. Just before he sailed he would have an advance. When he returned, he would come with his pockets jingling. Those times, the family lived well; but in between, Charles and his mother were at the mercy of London.

He tells one significant tale in his own story: when Sydney returned from his first trip with three pounds in tips, all in silver, Charles seized the money as Sydney poured it out on the counterpane, and he stacked it and rubbed it and stacked it again until his mother and Sydney called him a miser. He would never forget the feel of silver.

While Sydney was away on a voyage, their mother lost her sense of reality and was found one day wandering around Pownall Terrace, handing out pieces of coal to the children with assurance that they were 'gifts', and lamenting because 'they' were keeping Sydney away from her. That day Charles and the landlady took Hannah to the infirmary, where the doctor declared she was quite insane, and admitted her.

The small boy then lived a hunted existence, determined to keep out of the workhouse and the horrors of Hanwell. His mother was transferred back to Cane Hill Asylum, twenty miles away. The illness came when school was in holiday, but when the holidays ended, Charles still did not return. He made the acquaintance of some woodchoppers and they fed him, while he slept in the Pownall garret. He was only waiting for Sydney to come home, and when Sydney did come home to Waterloo Station, the dirty little urchin met him in a scene that might have been recreated years later in *The Kid.*

Sydney came home with a fortune—£20! He took Charles out the next day and bought him some clothes. They planned for the future. Both of them had decided to become actors, and they registered at Blackmore's Agency in the Strand.

Charles Chaplin's theatrical career now became a steady reality. He was signed to play the rôle of a newsboy in *Jim, the Romance of a Cockney,* for £2 10s. a week, and now he never looked back. *Jim* was less than a rousing success. It had a week at the Kingston theatre and a week at the Fulham, and was then consigned to oblivion. The *Topical Times* had little to say for the play but it had much to say for Charles Chaplin's spirited performance, and predicted a fine future for this child actor. He went on then, to the part of Billy the office boy in a production of *Sherlock Holmes.* This play was successful and was to provide employment for Chaplin for the next three years, but very little amusement. The youngest of the cast, he lived alone, and as they toured the provinces he occupied a series of bleak bedrooms, and walked the streets of one town after another, all alone. His one emotional contact was his brother Sydney, who had remained in London and secured a job as a bartender. In this period of melancholy, Charles Chaplin developed a new affection for his brother and a family closeness developed that was never to leave the pair. Also there came a shyness of manner that was to last many years, and often in the brilliant future to be misunderstood as arrogance. He was so shy that when the troupe's leading lady came upon him one day on the street and crossed to talk to him, he ducked down an alley so he would not have to face her. For a time he kept a rabbit, but one of his landladies put an end to that; the rabbit disappeared one day.

He met strange people and even freaks, and the experiences did not leave him. They were the 'little people' and for all the rest of his career, bits of his experience would find their way into his acting and later his motion pictures.

After nearly a year in the provinces, the company was given a brief respite in the suburbs of London, and Sydney got a part in the play. At the same time their mother came out of the asylum, but only briefly. Soon enough she was back in Cane Hill, and would remain hospitalized for all but the last few years of her life, when a wealthy Charlie would bring her to America.

The *Holmes* job lasted many months and was succeeded by an offshoot, *The Painful Predicament of Sherlock Holmes,* which opened at the Duke of York's Theatre on 3rd October 1905. Young Chaplin suffered his first case of puppy love for the leading actress, Marie Doro. She played in *Holmes,* but her meeting with young Chaplin were confined to encounters on the stairs, where she would wish the sixteen-year-old actor a good evening, and he would go away transported for the remainder of it.

Now names began to creep into Chaplin's cognizance. Before it had been the old beggar in Kennington Road, with bad feet and immense boots (he would lend his walk to the Charlie of the motion pictures) and the old blind musician outside the pub at Kennington Cross (he would help Chaplin form the image for the blind girl in *City Lights*). But now the name of Charles Frohman, the American impresario cropped up, and Miss Doro, and William Gillette, the actor and playwright, and Dion Boucicault. Queen Alexandra came to see the second *Holmes* play, and was seen by young Charles Chaplin. The King of Greece came, and so did Lord Kitchener. When the celebrated Sir Henry Irving died, actor Charles Chaplin attended the funeral at Westminster Abbey, by invitation. He was coming up in the world.

So cocky did Chaplin become in these weeks, that he turned down a chance to go on the road again and so when *Sherlock Holmes* ended its run at the Duke of York's Theatre, he was out of work. At the same time, the love of his young life, Marie Doro, went back to America. That night Chaplin's world came apart, and he said he went out alone and got desperately drunk. It was the first, and one of the few times, in his life.

For nearly a year the young actor was 'at liberty' living on his savings of the past and with Sydney who was employed soon by Fred Karno the impresario who sent so many troupes into the countryside. Sydney's troupe went out into the provinces too, and so Charles was left alone, to hang around the fringes of the theatrical community. He had half expected to be taken back to America with Gillette and Doro and so had not provided for the future. It was months before he found any steady work, and this in a vaudeville sketch, playing comedy rôles. In a way it was a comedown from the legitimate theatre of London's West End. In another way it was a step on the road of progression of Charles Chaplin's unique career. Out of necessity he created a burlesque of a celebrated character of the time, a 'Dr' Walford Bodie, the 'electrical wizard' and a patent medicine man. It caught on, and he was star of his show, earning £3 a week.

They called it Casey's Court Circus, and it cured for the moment the loneliness of the young actor. Half a dozen of the cast boarded in Kennington Road with a family named Fields. Young Chaplin fell in love with the fifteen-year-old daughter, but his intentions were anything but pure and she resisted him, so nothing came of the yearnings except, possibly, cold baths.

The Circus ended. Charles Chaplin was out of work again, but Sydney was working so he paid the bills and they both lived at the Fields's.

Until this time Chaplin's parts had been simple enough and usually set. He believed he was good enough at seventeen to launch into his own music-hall act, and he secured a week's trial without pay at a music hall in the Mile End Road, which was in the Jewish quarter of London. He tried to do a Jewish act, and it was such a complete failure on the first airing that he left the theatre amid jeers and catcalls, and never went back. At least he had learned something: he was not a Jewish comedian and never would be. He soon learned also that he was not a juvenile leading man, and he was not a comedy sketch author-director.

What he was he learned from Fred Karno, who was persuaded by Sydney to give the kid brother a chance in a slapstick sketch called *The Football Match*.

It had not been a very funny sketch, and its laughs were all reserved for Harry Weldon, a famous music-hall comedian. The man who had carried the part now assigned to young Chaplin had done nothing at all with it, and it was the success or failure of actors to embellish the basic Karno material that made the difference. Chaplin said he was scared stiff and he had no help; Sydney was off again in the provinces in another sketch, and Harry Weldon was so busy perfecting his golf game that he had no time to spare for a juvenile assistant.

Chaplin's costume consisted of a slouch hat, a huge black cape in which this slight youth nearly disappeared, and a little black moustache. He played a villain, whose task it was to persuade Goalkeeper Harry Weldon to throw the football match. The villain was first on stage, and given his chance for whatever laughs he might achieve by his performance. Then he was joined by Harry Weldon.

In previous weeks the villain's part had been flat, and there were no laughs until Weldon appeared. Chaplin's task was to change all that.

The scene was a gymnasium, with boxing paraphernalia

and exercise equipment scattered about.

Nervous as a cat on ice, Charles doctored up a huge red nose for himself, and then, on cue, he entered the stage with his back to the audience, then turned and showed his big red nose. Laugh No. 1.

He flitted across the stage gracefully (later John Barrymore would call him "the ballet dancer") only to trip over a dumb-bell. He had learned how many laughs could be secured from a walking stick in the Dr Bodie skit; now he used it again. His cane struck a punching bag, which hit him in the face. He fought back, and hit himself in the head with his cane. Laugh No. 2.

He manufactured other 'business'. A button came off and his trousers began to fall. More laughs.

He looked for the button and found rabbit droppings. Another laugh.

Harry Weldon came on, and the young actor nervously upstaged him by grabbing his arm and whispering, "Quick, I'm undone, a pin!" More laughs.

He was a success, and Weldon was a big enough star that he did not begrudge the young actor his due, but congratulated him. That night Charles Chaplin knew he was on his road. How lonely a road it would be for years also came to him that night, although he had no way of seeing into the future. There was no one to tell of his success; his mother was in the asylum, his brother on tour in the countryside. He stood on Westminster Bridge for a time, looking down into the dark waters of the Thames. He walked to the Elephant and Castle, alone, and then to Kennington Gate, and it was dawn before he got to bed.

3

The Music-Hall Entertainer

Whatever Harry Weldon thought of Charles Chaplin when the youngster added a new comedy element to the Karno skit, soon enough Weldon came to see the younger man as a definite threat. Chaplin was signed to a year's contract at £4 a week, hardly a threat to Weldon at more than £30 a week, but the older actor was soon feeling the strain. The act called for Weldon to knock Chaplin around the stage, and Weldon began to do so in earnest. One night, when Chaplin had received a particularly good review in the press, Weldon bloodied his nose, whereupon Chaplin threatened to retaliate with a dumb-bell next time.

But young Chaplin was on his way, and not a half dozen Harry Weldons could have stopped him. Soon he and young Arthur Stanley Jefferson were rising stars of the Karno organization. (Jefferson would go to America and become Stan Laurel.) Karno had some twenty skits that were alternated to fit audience tastes, and Chaplin played in many of them. Here he secured ideas that he would later adapt for the one-reelers when he went into motion pictures. He did acrobatics and miming, and tumbling and a little juggling —it was all part of the Karno technique. And he prospered.

Chaplin and Sydney moved to a flat in the Brixton Road, a large step upward from their previous lodgings, and they furnished it in some style, although their taste was rather rococo, with a nude pastel, a Moorish screen, an upright piano, two armchairs and a sofa. They were able to send money to their mother, and some to her father, who had fallen on difficult times. The days of poverty were gone forever.

Great changes were coming to London in this Edwardian

era, in which Charles Chaplin began to grow and flourish. The Balfour government moved to provide secondary education to English youth as a government responsibility. It meant nothing to this child of the slums who had virtually taught himself proficiency in reading and writing in that catch-as-catch-can education he had gone through. The Boer War brought newspaper headlines to London, but little else that captured the attention of the young Chaplin. He had been too immersed in poverty to care, and out of that stepped into the bathing pool of the theatre where he struggled to keep afloat and swim forward. He had no time at all to concern himself with public affairs, and by the time the Old Pension Law of 1909 offered his ageing grandfather a pension, he was so far removed from the past that even poverty was only an aching memory to him. The one aspect of the Edwardian era that did affect the young Chaplin was the general air of well-being that the pleasure-loving monarch brought to London, and the tremendous impetus which King Edward's interest lent the theatre in those carefree, happy days.

In his later teens, by his own account, Charles Chaplin developed into a libidinous youth. That strong sex drive would never leave him; in the years to come it would cause him untold difficulty and even agony in Puritan America. In that sense, Chaplin was born a half century too soon for America. But Edwardian London had none of those strictures, and among the free of heart, the theatrical crowd was nearly as unconscious of sexual *mores* as had been the Victorian poor among whom Chaplin grew up. He never lived and he never would live a conventional middle-class life anywhere; he was never middle-class, and that is what neither London nor Washington could quite understand about him. Unschooled in the usual sense, Chaplin did not develop any sense of English entity or British patriotism until later in life, and even then it seems to have been more a defensive gesture against American intrusions into his privacy than anything else. In his teens none of these problems bothered him, he was full of himself, and full of life, and at nineteen he fell in love.

The girl was named Hetty Kelly, and she was a song-

and-dance girl much like his mother had been, in a troupe
called Bert Coutts' Yankee Doodle Girls, playing at the
Streatham Empire. Chaplin's Karno troupe was playing
there too, and they met by chance when he held a mirror for
her. Chaplin was so smitten that he drew £3 out of the bank
to take her to the Trocadero, the most expensive restaurant
he knew. The evening was not very successful; the girl came
to Kennington Gate on the tramcar as she had promised, but
she had already eaten dinner, and he struggled through the
ceremonial service right down to the finger bowl, while she
toyed with a sandwich, to be polite. They walked to her
home in Camberwell. He got up at dawn the next day to
meet her before she had to go to rehearsals at eight. On the
fourth day he asked her if she loved him. He was
overwhelmed by her and by the power of his feelings. But she
was only fifteen and she honestly could not cope with such
extravagance, and so they parted, uncomfortably, and
anything but happily. For years Charles Chaplin would
recall Hetty Kelly. In later life he would talk about her a
good deal to writers and reporters and he would write about
her glowingly in his autobiography. Her effect was magnetic
and lasting; his whole relationship with women in the future
would be coloured by the memory of that fifteen-year-old
girl he had wanted so desperately to marry when he was
nineteen years old.

Luckily for Chaplin, the tragedy of this encounter was
soon wiped out by the excitement of his profession. He went
to Paris in 1909 when the *Folies Bergère* asked Karno for a
sketch. He was high-jacked by an expensive French prostitute for 20 francs and cabfare, and became involved with a
stage mother and her two talented daughters. The mother
and the elder daughter tried to seduce him, but so unwise in
the ways of the world was this twenty-year-old Lothario that
he did not really understand what was happening, and was
not caught up.

In Paris, Charles was exposed to Gallic culture and the
French way of life, and in years to come he would draw here
and there on the experience for his films. Some were
meaningless at the time, and would gather significance only
later, as his meeting Debussy, the composer, without know-

ing who he was. Debussy had seen the Karno sketch at the *Folies*, and came to compliment the young actor on skill and grace. Even at such a tender age, then, one genius recognized another. It was to be the pattern of Chaplin's lucky life. Karno knew, too.

The French episode ended in a month, and Charles was soon back in the provincial towns playing in one drab theatre after another to audiences whose basic idea of humour was a good pratfall. But Karno had not forgotten his young actor, and after a few months he offered Chaplin the starring rôle played earlier by Harry Weldon in *The Football Match*. It meant that for the first time his name would be featured at the top of the playbill. He was making £6 a week; now he could aspire to the £30 which was to Chaplin then a fortune.

For a moment Chaplin's luck deserted him. The show was to open at the Oxford Music Hall in London—definitely the big time. But before opening night Chaplin caught the 'flu and had laryngitis to boot. He struggled through mediocre performances until his understudy had to take over, the engagement was cut off at the end of a week, and fate had blown over his big chance.

Soon, however, Chaplin recovered from the illness and was again off into the provinces playing in *The Mumming Birds*, another Karno sketch. His part was that of a drunk who is supposedly not of the cast. He sits in a box and interrupts the show constantly with wild antics.

Charles elaborated on the part until it became the centre of the sketch. He would arrive in the theatre after the lights were down, and make his way noisily to the box in his dishevelled fancy clothes. On stage the players would quickly become annoyed and tell him to shut up or get out. He would challenge them and quarrel with them, while the singers, dancers, wrestlers and tumblers went about their acts. And finally, he would nearly fall out of the box, and pick a fight with 'The Terrible Turk' a strong man wrestler on the stage. The Turk would challenge him, and the slender, diminutive Charles would come down onto the stage drunkenly, and their 'fight' would be the climax to the act.

With such material, and with much success in the provinces, Charles Chaplin recovered the confidence that had been wiped out in that dreadful failure at the Oxford. But he remained a lonesome young man, spending hours trudging the streets of dingy, county towns, and walking forlornly in the parks. He was shy, and the life he led made him more so and extremely sensitive. One day in one of these towns, Chaplin discovered that another theatre housed a troupe with a number of young people in the cast. He decided to have a party for them in his room, after their evening performances were over. He cleaned the place himself, and bought flowers that afternoon and found vases for them, bought some cakes and sweets, found cups and a teapot and rushed back from the theatre that night and waited.

He waited an hour. He walked to the door and looked outside, and returned to his room and walked back to the door, and then back to the room again, his heart sinking more with each minute that passed. The young people never did come.

The manager of the troupe had heard of the party and stopped them. He said it was too late for them to go running across the town. Nobody had ever bothered to inform Charles Chaplin.

Such treatment made him a little bit more shy, a little more reserved than he had been before. It did not embitter him, he was always ready for a good joke.

The young Chaplin on tour was a late riser, and this caused the rest of the cast much worry from time to time. Their schedule called for them to arrive in a town on Sunday, and perform Monday through Saturday night, then to get the train on Sunday morning for their next town. Chaplin was the cross the road show-manager had to bear, for it always seemed nip and tuck whether he would arrive at the station on time to make the train. One Sunday when they had a very early train to catch—and there was no other—he nearly did miss it, and the manager then cautioned the others to be sure Chaplin was up and about on time.

All week long his fellow actors bedevilled him. On Sunday

morning, well before train time, they made sure he was awake. Someone came back ten minutes later. He was not up. The performance was repeated, and he still would not get up. The hands of the clock moved ominously forward, and the show manager in the hall consulted his watch. No Chaplin. He went upstairs. There was a tug of war with the bedclothes. Charles argued: he had never missed a train yet. The manager gave up, it was growing too late, and decided to leave Chaplin to his own devices.

As the manager clattered down the stairs, Chaplin sprang out of bed, fully clothed. He had got up early, and packed all his clothes, and now he seized the handbag, and hurried out, sprinted to the station, and waited there for the rest of the cast to arrive.

As a music-hall comedian, Charles Chaplin had not yet reached great heights in 1909; he was still the provincial player, feeling his way. He was not at all sure that he ever would become really first-rate in this line, and he worried about his prospects, because he had virtually no education. He was already reading voraciously. He was just about through his Schopenhauer period, but his reading was catch-as-catch-can, depending on what struck his fancy, or what author's name had been dropped by someone he respected.

Renewed success with *The Mumming Birds* and several other sketches brought Chaplin's flagging fortunes back to normal, but he was still edgy in the spring of 1910, when Alf Reeves, the manager of Karno's American company came to recruit new talent for the following season. He came up to Birmingham, where Charles Chaplin was appearing in a sketch, and wired Karno that he wanted to take Chaplin back with him.

Karno was not enthusiastic. Chaplin was just then appearing in a sketch called *Skating,* and Karno did not believe it would go over in the States. But at the same time, in London, he was experimenting with a sketch called *The Wow-Wows,* a parody of an American college-fraternity or secret-society initiation. Karno believed it was fatuous enough to appeal to the American audience, and he and Reeves agreed that young Chaplin should have the major rôle. Charles had been wanting to go to America for some time, not at all satisfied that his future lay in England. Now he was to have his chance.

4

America

In the summer of 1910 the decision was made. Charles Chaplin would accompany Alf Reeves and his wife back to the United States and join the Karno travelling company there.

The twenty-one-year-old Chaplin had decided, before he sailed, that if possible he would cast his lot with the United States. He knew virtually nothing about the place, except that it was large and open, and that the future was bright for people who had not been able to make a success in the old countries. Chaplin was going through a period of introspection, and he was certain that his lack of education and breeding would keep him from ever rising higher than the music hall circuit in London. He told no one, not even Sydney. One night he took one of his long exhausting evening walks around the West End, and said his private good-byes. Next morning, he left a note for Sydney, and was gone bright and early to the station to begin his journey overseas.

It was a measure of his station, and that of the Karno company, that they travelled on a cattle boat, not an ocean liner. It was summer, but they encountered storms, and the crossing was so cold they bundled up in their overcoats to go on deck.

But America was warm, from the time they hit Toronto. Soon enough they were in New York, and immediately Chaplin felt at home, and reaffirmed his intention to remain in this bustling country if he could manage it. It was not at all certain in the beginning.

The American comic tradition was only distantly related to the English. Vaudeville was the closest equivalent to the

English music-hall comedy, and vaudeville had developed in America in its unique way, with strong infusions from Negro, Jewish, and Irish humour, song, and dance. The slapstick (which made a noise like a shot) and the pratfall were standard items of humour. Few turns depended on wit and the spoken word. 'Business' was more important than talk, although there were patter artists such as Joe Cook, and Weber and Fields combined the slapstick with their jokes to reach success. There were clowns and monologue artists, and singers and dancers. W. C. Fields was in his prime, with his insane combination of juggling and gentlemanly mayhem. Jimmy Durante was at work, so were Al Jolson and a young George Burns, and the Marx Brothers family act was on the boards.

Charles Chaplin began in America under a shadow. Alf Reeves had known from experience that *The Wow Wows* was not going to 'wow' an American audience. Chaplin had sensed it from the beginning. Both had argued with Fred Karno in favour of one of several other sketches, but Karno was a stubborn boss, and he insisted that he knew the market better than they.

Chaplin played a character named Archie. In the opening of the skit he came out from a tent into a camping scene with a teacup asking for water, because he wanted to take a bath.

That opening had brought down the English houses. It was greeted in stony silence by American audiences. (Perhaps the English did take baths in teacups, how were they to know? The ways of foreigners were beyond comprehension.)

There was no saving of the laughter, it just would not come. The differences of language and tempo of speech were such that much of the dialogue went completely over the heads of the Americans. *The Wow-Wows* was a dismal flop on the Percy Williams circuit.

They opened on 3rd October at the Colonial Theatre in New York. The whole booking was only for six weeks, scarcely enough for a foreign impresario to dispatch a company. But Karno had a mighty reputation in America, and in earlier times there had always been plenty of bookings to supplement the original. *The Wow-Wows*—that was something else again.

Chaplin was reviewed most sympathetically, ". . . typically English, the sort of comedian that American audiences seem to like . . . his manner is quiet and easy and he goes about his work in a devil-may-care manner . . . Chaplin will do all right for America". That comment was in *Variety,* one of the most important of the theatrical trade journals.

A week later the show was in Brooklyn, where the reception was just as dismal, so dreadful that Chaplin hated to go on and face the people. Performing was worse than drudgery, it was embarrassing, and it continued to be embarrassing for the six weeks. The only compensation was Charles Chaplin's discovery of America.

Wherever he went, he walked. He got to know Times Square, and he walked on Fifth Avenue, along Millionaires Row where the nabobs lived. But he also walked to The Bowery and to the lower East Side which spawned and spewed forth the children of the refugees who had come here to seek their pots of gold. He felt the increased tempo of life, and he saw the Americans trying this line of work and that one, never afraid to change, always looking for the way to make the 'fast buck'. Chaplin was not so sure of the theatre or of himself that he had any plans for the future—except that he wanted to stay on in America and make his fortune.

In the third week, the troupe played the Fifth Avenue Theater, and found for the first time an audience that understood and appreciated the music-hall turns. Most of those in the audience were English, waiters and butlers and other servants of the well-to-do. The players were lucky—an agent for a third-rate string of vaudeville houses caught the act before a responsive audience, and booked the troupe for a twenty-week tour of the West.

So they went on tour. Life was so cheap in the West in 1910 that Chaplin lived well on $25 a week and paid his own lodgings. He saved $50 every week, and was soon talking about abandoning the theatrical world and becoming a hog farmer, an enthusiasm that lasted until he learned about hogs.

They travelled to Chicago, up to Minneapolis, down to St Louis, west to Kansas City and Denver and Butte, which had the most highly touted red-light district in the West. It was, of course, the after-hours milieu of the theatrical people, for in America as in England, actors and actresses in particular were beyond the pale of polite society. They went west to California, still playing *The Wow-Wows*. Early in 1911 they were back in New York, and apparently heading home to England, with no more than indifferent success. But William Morris, the theatre owner, somehow learned that the Karno troupe had better acts in its repertoire and engaged them to play a number of different sketches for six weeks in New York.

Chaplin made his mark on New York in *A Night in an English Music Hall*, which was essentially *The Mumming Birds* again, except that in this version the whole Music Hall, stage to boxes, was transported to the American stage. Chaplin was the drunk in the evening dress who interrupted the performance with all those turns and gestures he had learned so well in the English provinces. His humour depended more and more on sight gags and 'business' and the American audiences began to pack the house. So successful was *A Night in an English Music Hall* that the Karno troupe secured still another booking on the western circuit and so Chaplin and his friends went west for twenty weeks more.

Then it was back to London. Chaplin had looked forward to getting home, to the comfortable flat on Brixton Road, but when he got to London everything had changed. Sydney had got married, and moved out of the flat. Their mother was still in an institution. Although England welcomed with her finest weather in this spring of 1912, Chaplin's loneliness and dissatisfaction were heavy burdens for him to bear. His dreams returned him to America. In his autobiography, Chaplin refers to an incident that expressed one of his major reasons for wanting to make the change. He had gone to visit Fred Karno in the country. Karno, an old entertainer, was now a wealthy man and he maintained a luxurious, showy houseboat at Tagg's Island. Chaplin was sitting on deck with his host and hostess after dinner, when a boat came by bearing a man and woman of the upper class, who laughed and made insulting remarks about the garishness of the houseboat. To Chaplin, this gesture typified all that he disliked about England; as long as he would remain in the

English isles, no matter how much money he made, the world would not let him forget the poverty of his beginnings. In America a boy could be born and grow up on the 'wrong side' of the tracks, but he could become an American gentleman. It was money and power that counted, not class. Chaplin had enjoyed a good season in America. He obviously sensed that he would be welcomed back there again. His talent would bring him money, and money would bring him power. And together they should bring him happiness.

All along he had felt that he was going back to America, and now after several months in the provinces, the electrifying word came: the troupe had been signed for another tour of the American West.

Back they went, this time on a liner travelling second class, which was an improvement on the first voyage. And back to the lonely life of the young performer on the vaudeville circuit. They played the suburbs of the big eastern cities for a time, and Charles occupied a series of dismal rooms. He might have doubled up with a roommate, but he was shy, and also he liked doing things his own way. He began reading again, determined to acquire a veneer of culture that would hide the wretchedness he felt about his humble beginnings. He continued to dip into Schopenhauer, and he read some Emerson, some Poe, some Hawthorne, and bits and pieces of other writers. Probably he read enough to be able to pass off a few quotations and aphorisms. He was not reading as a serious student; his ideas and his art came from the world he had seen and heard and felt himself.

Midway in 1913 the Karno American troupe was resting in Philadelphia for a week before heading west, when Alf Reeves received a telegram from New York.

Did he have an actor named Charlie Chapman working for him? If so, would Chapman get in touch with Kessel and Baumann in their office building on Broadway.

There was no Chapman. But on the hope that they might have meant Chaplin, and that he might be a secret heir to millions, Charles wired back, and was invited to New York.

In New York, Chaplin discovered that Kessel and Baumann were not lawyers, but the owners of several motion picture ventures, including Keystone comedies. Mack Sennett, the producer of the comedies, had recently been having some salary difficulties with his major star, Ford Sterling. He wanted to back up his stable of actors with more talent, and he thought of the funny little English actor he had seen the year before at a performance of *A Night in an English Music Hall.*

"He could make you laugh till you cried," said Sennett, when he had recommended Chaplin to his associates.

Chaplin was not overwhelmed by Keystone comedies. They were almost pure slapstick, but as the world knew they were immensely popular. Besides, Kessel offered him $150 a week, which was just twice that he was making with Karno. And they would wait until he finished his Karno bookings.

That innate bookkeeping sense came to the fore, and Kessel managed to better the contract a little, $150 for the first three months, and then $175 for the rest of the year. Chaplin accepted, and in November he played his last performance at the Empress Theater in Kansas City, and headed west, while the troupe went home to England. That last night was a solemn one for the young actor, who at twenty-three was cutting the only real ties he had.

Will Murray's 'Casey's Court', 1906, Chaplin fourth from the right, middle row and (*below*) Brixton Road at the time of Chaplin's childhood

A Karno poster, Chaplin third from the top, and (*right*) Marie Doro, leading actress in *The Painful Predicament of Sherlock Holmes*, 1905, and the object of Chaplin's 'puppy love'

Charlie Chaplin in 1914, and (*right*) the house in which he lived in Kennington Road

(*Left to right*) Grice, Chaplin, Mack Sennett and D. W. Griffith and (*right*) Charlie and Sydney Chaplin in 1921

A scene from *Tillie's Punctured Romance:* Marie Dressler rampages while Chaplin and Mabel Normand hide behind the curtain

Chaplin as boxer, taken on the set of *City Lights* and (*below, left to right*) Mary Pickford, D. W. Griffith, Chaplin and Douglas Fairbanks Snr, 1919

The Kid

The Gold Rush: Chaplin with Black Larsen and Big Jim McKay

Chaplin sees his wife, Lita,
off on a trip to Honolulu,
with their son,
Charles, 1926

Lita Grey Chaplin, at the
time of her divorce, with
her mother, grandfather,
and her two sons, Charles
and Sydney

Chaplin arrives at
Paddington Station during
his trip to England in 1931

Chaplin with Pola Negri

5

The Motion Pictures

Charles Chaplin entered the motion-picture world under a cloud. He arrived in Los Angeles, put at a cheap hotel, and on the first evening went to the show at the Empress Theater, where he had worked earlier with the Karno troupe. There he met, quite by accident, Mack Sennett and Mabel Normand, and when Sennett set eyes on the twenty-three-year old Englishman he had hired by telegraph, the producer was afraid he had made a serious mistake.

Sennett originated American film comedy in his own folk image. He was a big Irishman from Canada, and his ideal of humour was a chase, a kick, and a pratfall, followed by a custard pie in someone's face. He had learned the film art from the great D. W. Griffith at Biograph, and then had branched off on his own. For more than a year he had been making successful slapstick comedies with Ford Sterling, Mabel Normand, Fatty Arbuckle, Mack Swain, and the famous Keystone Cops. He was the master of an art about which Chaplin knew nothing.

Charles Chaplin was painfully aware that the first impression he had left on Sennett was not favourable. Nervous as he had ever been before a performance, he took a streetcar next day to the suburban Los Angeles site of the Keystone lot, located on an abandoned farm, with an old one-storey house as the office. He was so shy and so overwhelmed that he stood around for a few minutes, and when neither Sennett nor Miss Normand appeared, he got back on a streetcar and went to the hotel. It was three days before he appeared on the lot.

Sennett then took Chaplin around to the studio, which was an open platform hung high horizontally with muslin sheets to diffuse the sunlight. Several comedies were being made at once, each with its own set, stage hands, cameramen, actors, and directors. To one uninitiated it sounded and looked like total confusion.

As they toured, Sennett explained a little of his philosophy of motion-picture making to Chaplin, who found the central idea of the chase most distasteful. He said nothing, but already a problem had been created.

Sennett was obviously queasy about what use to make of his latest acquisition. Ford Sterling would be leaving soon to form his own company, and Chaplin had to be broken in. After a few days of gawking Chaplin was ready, but Sennett was busy with other affairs. It was two weeks before any thing happened, and then it occurred in a roundabout fashion. Sennett and most of the rest of the crew went off on location. Director Henry Lehrman was in charge of the studio, and he needed an actor to play a newspaper reporter. Chaplin was available, so he became the reporter.

He dressed in the same basic costume he had used for *A Night in an English Music Hall*—frock coat, high silk hat, walrus moustache and monacle. Then he was ready.

There was no plot. They were to make up the story as they went along, and they did, finishing the filming in three days. Chaplin did not like the frenetic pace of the Keystone operation, and tried to slow down the film with his own bits of characterization. He and Lehrman clashed several times about the manner in which a certain action should be taken. And then there was the additional difficulty that Chaplin did not understand the film process. For example, a sequence was shot of Chaplin looking at Virginia Kirtely, his leading lady in the film. When it was finished, Lehrman ordered the camera to a different position. He also ordered Chaplin to gaze in a certain direction, and pretend he was looking at the girl. Chaplin objected. He could not see the girl, he said. Lehrman had to stop and explain to him the process of film editing, and the usefulness of having shots from several angles to intercut into the action. Chaplin did not much appreciate the advice, and Lehrman did not much appreciate giving it to the 'limey'.

Once the film was shot, Lehrman proceeded to edit it.

By this time, Sennett and the others were back from location, and they went into the screening room to see what the new actor had done.

Sennett groaned. Now he was certain he had made a dreadful error in hiring the little Englishman. Mabel Normand said he was a "package mis-sent". Lehrman said he was not easy to work with; he seemed to argue all the time, and had insisted on slowing down the whole pace of the film so that he could get in his 'characterizations'.

It was a basic difference of approach. As edited, the film pleased none of them. Sennett and Lehrman thought it was too slow; Chaplin said Lehrman had butchered his best bits.

But good or bad, it was finished. The ravenous maw of the burgeoning motion-picture demanded product and more product. Making a Living it was titled, and released early in 1914. If it flopped, so would Chaplin.

Sennett was leery about using his new actor, so Chaplin was again assigned to Lehrman, and sent out to a children's auto race at Venice, a California seaside resort near Los Angeles. Sennett got his crowd effects from real crowds, using any kind of an event as a backdrop for his comedy.

Chaplin was told to abandon his dude outfit and put on a funny costume. He shared dressing space in a big barn with most of the other featured Sennett players, and in the dressing room he looked about for comedy props. Fatty Arbuckle was a fat man: he took a pair of Arbuckle's pants, which were much too large for him. Ford Sterling wore a size 14 shoe; he took Sterling's shoes, and wore them on the wrong feet so they would stay on. He found a coat two sizes too small for himself, and a derby one size too small, and he cut down one of Mack Swain's big moustaches to toothbrush moustache size. Then he picked up a small bamboo cane, and lo, a character was born.

As he dressed the character came to him, straight out of the streets of poverty. It was to be a combination of a dude and a bum, a gentle fellow down on his luck, a tramp with the soul of a poet.

Then he and Lehrman went out to film Kid Auto Races at Venice. A prop camera was set up in front of the real one, and the tramp made a nuisance of himself running out on the race track and getting in the way of the camera. He walked like an injured duck, he bumped into the cameraman and then upbraided him, and then they brawled in the best Sennett manner. The Keystone Cops showed up and tried to get him out of the way. He resisted, and brawled some more.

It was a very short film. Sennett was not taking any chances on losing money on the unknown and debatable addition to his studio. It was, in fact, only half of one reel, the other half being a documentary short on the making of olive oil. And yet, this was the beginning of Charlie.

6

The Comedy

All that had gone before December 1913 was simply preparation. The years in the theatrical ambience, the tours of the music halls, the failure and poverty in which he grew up, and all the sad, sick, tired, beaten characters who had crossed his path were a part of the character that would first be called 'the tramp', and would end up becoming 'the little fellow'.

Robert Payne suggested that Chaplin derived the character from a town councillor in the Island of Jersey in the summer of 1912, when Chaplin visited the island. Chaplin watched the man directing a parade. He was an absurd figure in the first place, and he insinuated himself in front of the camera, somehow managing to push all others aside, until the newsreel cameraman who was filming the parade erupted in anger. The councilman continued to smile, wave, pirouette, and smile some more. This was the image that came to Chaplin's mind when he and director Lehrman set up camera to work their film into the auto races. As he worked, he thought of the Jersey councilman and tried to be as obnoxiously obtrusive.

That character was not yet Charlie, the waif who won the hearts of the world. It was not yet even the tramp, a not entirely lovable figure, with whom Chaplin would begin. But the props were there, and the building had begun. Chaplin had learned on his first day of work that the toff figure he had played so successfully in the music halls would not do for America.

In his study of the art of the silent-movie comedians, Walter Kerr has concluded that Chaplin suffered "the hopeless limitation of having no limitations". Chaplin was the consummate actor, he could play any role.

In that Keystone comedy, the Chaplin role was extremely limited. The tramp figure in the beginning was not allowed much time for his 'business' of setting character.

Next day Lehrman was assigned to make a new picture, starring Mabel Normand, but Chaplin was left on the sideline with nothing to do. He came to the studio that day and went up on to the set to watch. Sennett came up with Miss Normand, and spotted Chaplin. Apparently he had screened the Venice race film and found it more to his liking, for he told Charles to get into a comedy make-up. Chaplin went to the dressing room and put on his Charlie make-up again.

The set simulated a hotel lobby. Charlie shuffled into the lobby, in his ridiculous costume, trying to look like a guest, failing miserably, and knowing it all the while. He went to the telephone, and fumbled for a coin. No coin.

At bay, he turned, and stumbled over the foot of a lady. Politely he raised his hat. He stumbled over a cuspidor. Again he raised his hat. . . .

As Charles worked at the characterization, the other actors, stagehands, and crew members clustered around to watch. Ford Sterling stood there. So did Fatty Arbuckle. All the lot knew of the tension that existed between the new comedian and the management, and all wanted to see what was going to happen to him under the eyes of the big boss.

When Chaplin tipped his hat to the cuspidor, he got a laugh. When Mabel entered with a dog on a leash, with unerring inaccuracy, the tramp was immediately tangled up with the dog, fell, and got his hand stuck in the cuspidor. There were more laughs.

Chaplin was then scolded by the hotel desk clerk, and he mugged and twisted and turned and got more laughs—these from people who worked with comedy every day.

Even Mack Sennett was laughing by this time, and the tension was broken.

The comedy that was titled *Mabel's Strange Predicament* was not Sennett's usual kind of film, but since he knew that Chaplin had added an element Sennett was willing to gamble. Chaplin was even allowed to have his own way in some aspects. That hotel lobby scene would normally have been cut to ten feet of film, but Chaplin persuaded Sennett to let it run the full seventy-five feet. He did not lose any of his 'business' the way he had in *Making A Living*.

The critic of *Moving Picture World* liked *Making a Living*, and called Chaplin a first-rate comedian, even without the tramp characterization. That review helped, and it came at a critical time. Lehrman, was still not very much impressed with him, and was not inclined to accept any advice on film-making from the young Englishman. Chaplin was an opinionated young man, and he spent a considerable amount of time arguing about what he wanted to do. The Sennett humour was confined to a sort of organized violence on the screen, and really nothing else was wanted.

In *Mabel's Strange Predicament*, Chaplin really proved to Mack Sennett and the others that he was as funny as Sennett had originally believed him to be. That acceptance secured Chaplin the third film, another one-reeler called *Between Showers*, in which he and Ford Sterling quarrelled over which of them is to help the chubby Emma Clifton over a large puddle, and then got into a typical Sennett scuffle over an umbrella.

Between Showers was typical of the early Chaplin films in one respect. They were sketches on the screen, not so much different from the type of rôle that Chaplin was used to playing in the music halls.

In the first few weeks after he was hired and accepted as competent, Chaplin worked with Sennett for the most part, after the other directors indicated he was too hard to handle. The character was funny in the Sennett sense, but hardly endearing. In *Tango Tangles* he fought with Fatty Arbuckle and Ford Sterling over the affections of a hat-check girl. In *His Favorite Pastime* he got drunk in a saloon and annoyed the customers and then followed a girl home, to be accosted by her husband.

In the beginning, the tramp figure was not totally established. For Chaplin's eighth film he went back to the toff figure once more. This one-reeler featured Charles Chaplin as Lord Helpus, with the dapper clothes, cane, and walrus moustache. He was back to the tramp in the next one, as a boarder who won the affection of his landlady much to the husband's annoyance. Edgar Kennedy played the husband, and Alice Davenport the landlady. Chaplin was able in this picture to keep in a fairly lengthy scene of himself and the landlady playing tennis, which was quite a departure from the usual Sennett technique.

The tenth picture marked the crisis in Chaplin's relations with Sennett. Mabel Normand began the direction, and she and Chaplin quarrelled when he wanted to add bits of 'business' that she declared would do nothing but slow down the film. Sennett resolved the difficulties and they made a two-reeler out of it, *Mabel at the Wheel.* Chaplin's character was still not fixed; in this motion picture he wore a frock coat, high hat, a moustache and chin whiskers. The character was the obnoxious interferer.

While they were quarrelling, he did *Twenty Minutes of Love* with Edgar Kennedy, Minta Durfee and Chester Conklin; more of the usual slapstick, with everyone ending up in a lake.

Then came the crisis: when Chaplin was about to be fired by Sennett the word came from New York that the Chaplin pictures were catching on. The next film brought back the tramp to stay. Charles Chaplin won the right to have a say in the direction, and Sennett announced to the world that the film *Caught in a Cabaret* was the first of a new series to star the young English actor.

When Chaplin was thus secure, he and Mabel Normand managed to work together as a directing and acting team in several pictures. He also appeared as a bit player in Fatty Arbuckle's *The Knockout,* but Mabel was not a bit player. For the first few motion pictures they made together she insisted that she be co-director. It was only after the Chaplin pictures had achieved great success that she was willing to let him direct her.

Although Chaplin was credited with writing and directing the films at Keystone, what little writing was done was apparently on the backs of envelopes. The director and cast would assemble with a camera and a central theme. It was so simple an operation that when Charles later tried to persuade his brother Sydney to join him in a venture, he spoke of needing only a camera and a lot somewhere.

That assessment was not precisely correct at Keystone, where he must still remain within the limits of the Sennett action formula. After the initial clashes, he and Sennett got on well; they spent part of nearly every day together, talking over ideas for films, both Chaplin's and those of the other players.

From the beginning Chaplin observed that the Keystone players and directors had much to gain from the theatre. He had learned; long before the music-hall sketches, he had played in the theatre of the West End. So he knew a good deal about techniques. There was a lot of walking in Sennett films; walking was not dramatic. The comedians, most of whom had practised the new art by experiment, did not know much about pantomime. Chaplin taught them some things, and learned a lot himself, particularly about film editing, which was as important as the filming itself.

In Chaplin's twelfth film, *Caught in a Cabaret,* he persuaded co-director Normand to adopt some of the English music-hall comedy technique. In this film Chaplin impersonated a duke and flirted with Miss Normand at a garden party. He was nearly exposed when he crossed his legs and showed a hole in the bottom of his shoe. Quick! The hat was off the head and on to the toe of the shoe. That was typical Chaplin business. But the film was also full of puns, which, of course, were delivered in subtitles written on the screen.

Here are two:

After Charlie had fought off a bully in her defence, Mabel Normand asked him to her house "for a *tête-à-tête*".

"Certainly if you have any on ice," said the duke.

Chaplin identified himself as O. T. Axle, Ambassador for Greece. (In reality the 'duke' was a waiter in a cheap restaurant.)

"Fancy a real *Ambassador,*" said Miss Normand. "He must be the man all the hotels are named after."

The punning was suspended and the slapstick taken up, with Chaplin making frantic love to Miss Normand, putting his arm on her bosom, and throwing his leg over her lap (in a manner that Groucho Marx was to perfect).

But the puns came again.

"Nothing but the affairs of Greece would take me away from you tonight", said Chaplin. Next he was seen as a drudge in the cheap restaurant.

When the others from the garden party went slumming and arrived at the restaurant, Chaplin was ordered to serve them and did, spilling wine and food all over Miss Normand's suitor, and knocking Miss Normand down. Then in came the custard pies (a technique invented by Miss Normand) and more slapstick until the end—which was Chaplin's, right out of the music halls.

At the finale of the picture, Chaplin was in Miss Normand's arms, and he looked at her soulfully.

"I may be only a waiter," he said, "but remember Bismarck was only a herring."

Chaplin was having at least part of his way.

One reel or two, these films averaged about one a week in the shooting and editing, and not so many of them are notable for the punning as for the slapstick. Chaplin was being held down; he was learning that puns are more English than American and he was developing the character that he portrayed on the screen. In his study of comedy, Robert Payne says it was just after *Caught in a Cabaret* that Chaplin exhibited the full force of the character for a fleeting moment. It came in *Caught in the Rain,* his next picture and the first that he directed himself.

Chaplin, playing the tramp, met Alice Davenport in the park and began to make approaches. He smiled, behaved like a bird doing a mating dance, and invited her to sit on a bench with him. Along came Mack Swain, her husband, and threw Chaplin into the bushes, nearly destroying his precious hat. They left Chaplin, and Chaplin wandered back to the hotel and into the wrong room. Of course it was the lady's room and the husband again threw Chaplin out bodily. He went to his own room next door, lay down fully dressed and pulled the bedclothes over him, then thumbed his nose at the room next door.

The lady came 'sleepwalking' into his room, arms outstretched. And here Chaplin extended himself. In a brief moment, his features and actions represented desire, fear of the husband, and contempt. Then she sat beside him, and her hand groped for his wallet. . . .

The rest was pure Mack Sennett. The husband found them together, and this time Chaplin was thrown out of the hotel into the rain, and the chase began, complete with Keystone Cops. But for that moment, the world had been offered a glimpse of the new character that was building within the heart and mind of Charles Chaplin.

Most of the thirty-five films Chaplin made for Keystone in that one year were the same combination of Sennett's technique and Chaplin's growing sense of his own. At first, the Chaplin character wobbled, and he experimented with props, but by the end of the year the Charlie figure was set. The style of the character varied widely in the Keystone films, but basically he was a tramp, with a tramp's disregard for law and convention. There was never any effort made by Sennett and his troupe to enlist audience sympathy: the Keystone comedies were to be laughed at, not with, and Chaplin's films followed this basic line, although from time to time Chaplin introduced a turn that did play for audience sympathy. At his worst the tramp could be quite a fiendish fellow: in *The Property Man,* Chaplin made an old prop man carry a heavy trunk, kicked the old man in the face, and sat on the trunk when the old man collapsed under the weight. He was hardly the woeful figure of *City Lights,* but he made the cinema public laugh.

The important aspect of the Chaplin one- and two-reelers for Keystone was the opportunity they gave him to exercise his wit. One must assume from the record that Sennett and his assistants simply announced to Chaplin: "All right, now be funny", and that the bits and pieces of comic art that Chaplin exhibited were his own. Few of the other comics had more than one basic theme. Edgar Kennedy, for example, was the master of the 'slow burn' in which he registered surprise, incredulity, annoyance, and finally fury which erupted in some sort of violence.

All that Sennett really wanted was the basic action. It was enough that Chaplin developed the penguin shuffle, the acrobatic cane, the wriggling moustache, and a trick of sliding around corners on one splayed shoe, while the other leg stuck out. Add to that the chase, a drunk act, a quarrel over a girl, violence and the custard pie, and you had a film. Given his own way, Chaplin accepted this approach, and then improvised.

He added the trash can as a basic prop. Sometimes he hid in it, sometimes he slept in it. Once he kneeled next to it and prayed. He added the knee-slapping routine; talking to a prospective employer about a job he started slapping the other's knee. The other man moved his leg and Chaplin slapped again, nearly capsized, and then pulled back. In *The New Janitor,* Chaplin at one point was given a wad of banknotes. He counted them carefully, and only after counting did he thank his benefactor. There was a scene that somehow took one back to a five-year-old Chaplin collecting coins on stage after his first public appearance, and then following the helping stage manager exit to be sure he did not make off with the collection.

The point is, of course, that Chaplin used everything he ever saw, everything he ever did; he extracted bits from his observations and from his own character, and he was as ruthless in finding himself as he was in exposing the absurdities of others. The sudden rages of the tramp were pure Chaplin, and they were to be duplicated in life, as were the abrupt turns from rage to tenderness. In *His Trysting Place,* Chaplin was married to Mabel Normand, and they had a baby. He forgot to feed the baby and carried it about as if it were a toy, not real. He got his coat mixed up with Mack Swain's in a restaurant, and Mabel found a note from a woman in the coat he wore home. She broke an ironing board over his head and pushed him into an ashcan. He went into the park and sobbed; that was another Chaplin, much nearer to the Charlie who would be so abused by the world.

The progress was slow but sure. By the time he made his twenty-seventh film, *The New Janitor,* Chaplin was becoming sure of his direction, and he had added much to the dimension of film comedy on the Keystone lot. When he was making that film, he said, an old time actress stood on the lot and wept at the scene in which the janitor was fired, and tried to rescue his job by appealing that he had a large family of small children to support. No one ever wept at Edgar Kennedy wiping the slow burn off his face. Chaplin was discovering that he could keep an audience between tears and laughter.

Near the end of Chaplin's year with Keystone, he became involved in a significant new venture, a six-reel feature film, which Sennett, considering it so important, directed himself. The film was *Tillie's Punctured Romance,* and unlike most Sennett comedies it was an adaptation of the stage play *Tillie's Nightmare,* in which Marie Dressler starred on Broadway. Miss Dressler was chosen to star in the same role in the film, and Chaplin was selected as the male lead. Most of Keystone's important actors played in this film too: Mabel Normand, Mack Swain, Chester Conklin, Edgar Kennedy, Charley Chase, Minta Durfee, Alice Davenport, Alice Howell, and the Keystone Cops were all a part of it.

The scenario was written by Hampton Del Ruth. It was a big Sennett undertaking, and Chaplin's role was only as an actor. Yet so important was the film to Chaplin's career, that biographer Theodore Huff has said it was responsible for Chaplin's name becoming known to the general motion picture public. One reason for this was that most Keystone comedies did not celebrate the players with a billing; millions knew the Chaplin tramp but not the name.

The film began with Chaplin, the city slicker, looking for country victims. He found them in the 18 stone of Miss Dressler, who was more than twice Chaplin's size, and Mack Swain, her farmer father. Miss Dressler opened the romance by hitting Chaplin with a brick by mistake, then taking him home for resuscitation. So far it was pure Mack Sennett. Chaplin managed to work in his own art at length in a scene on a high fence, where he tried to make love to Miss Dressler while balancing himself precariously. This brought into play several of Chaplin's artistic qualities, not the least of which was his skill as an acrobat. From the beginning, Chaplin had been the master of the trip and the fall and the recovery. These assets were derived from his music-hall days, when he had learned the art of falling without getting hurt. He had already taught this technique to the Sennett crowd, now he exhibited it in a new context.

Chaplin persuaded Miss Dressler to steal her father's money and run away with him to the city, and there they were nearly killed in traffic (typical Sennett byplay) and espied by Mabel Normand, who played Chaplin's partner in crime. Miss Normand knocked Chaplin down, he was rescued by Miss Dressler. Next, in a café, Miss Dressler drank too much and, being tipsy, insisted on dancing. She fell down, and not even five men could pick her up. Chaplin, meanwhile, had disappeared with Miss Normand and Miss Dressler's purse with the money in it. Miss Dressler was jailed for her antics, but bailed out by a rich uncle, a man so virtuous he would not see his erring niece. But very quickly the uncle was jettisoned he went climbing a mountain and fell into a crevasse.

Naturally, in the comic tradition, Miss Dressler inherited a huge fortune. Chaplin and Miss Normand had been living high on Miss Dressler's money, but when Chaplin saw the headline in the papers about a really large fortune, he deserted Miss Normand on a park bench and found Miss Dressler, rushing her to a minister, and marrying her.

In this sequence there were elements of the original Broadway show, elements of Sennett, and some of Chaplin, all mixed together. After losing her money, Miss Dressler got a job as a waitress; Chaplin and Miss Normand came in, and in the confrontation she dropped her tray of dishes on his head and fainted. That is almost pure Sennett. In the scene on the park bench with Miss Normand, Chaplin had 'business' with the newspapers. That is Chaplin. On his way to find Miss Dressler and get her to the preacher, Chaplin turned corners with his little skid turn, and knocked over people right and left. That was Sennett modified by Chaplin. With the preacher, somehow the telephone directory was substituted for the Bible. That was Chaplin again.

After the wedding, Chaplin and Miss Dressler moved into the dead uncle's mansion, an overdecorated house that symbolized the new rich, with servants in livery and powdered wigs, standing in two long rows to greet them. Now Chaplin had it all to himself. He hung his hat and cane on the butlers, and marched up and down surveying them as he would a line of cattle. The scene ran long enough to give a real impact. It ended with Chaplin losing his dignity in exiting, when he tripped on the rug.

Most of the picture, however, was Miss Dressler's. She was the Broadway star, and Sennett let her have the big scenes. She chased Chaplin around the house with a gun when she discovered the new maid was Mabel Normand, and Chaplin kissing her. She threw pies. She danced wild dances. She went after Chaplin in pure Sennett style, found him hiding in a big vase, broke the vase and began choking him—just as 'dead' Uncle appeared, having escaped from the crevasse. Uncle threw them all out of his house, and the scene changed to the Sennett chase, the Keystone Cops came in and Chaplin, Miss Dressler and Miss Normand ended up at the beach in the water, avoiding boats and clinging to piers.

Although the picture was largely Miss Dressler's down to the last scene, where Chaplin has been discarded by both women, there Chaplin had another bit that was to be so much a part of the Charlie story. As the women were consoling one another, and upbraiding the city slicker, he shrugged off the whole affair and both of them with that little philosophic gesture, just as the Keystone Cops came to drag him away. There was a glimpse of the indestructible little fellow who would never win, but somehow would come back to fight again.

Tillie's Punctured Romance was begun in April 1914, after Chaplin had been on the Keystone lot long enough to prove himself. By the time it was released in November, the public had become very much aware of the odd pasty-faced little clown, and so he offered them a familiar face, and familiar routines. Of course, Miss Dressler was already widely known and it was her film. The combination of the familiar Keystone figures and Miss Dressler's elephantine romping made just the kind of humour that America demanded at the moment, and the film was extremely successful. The reviewers generally acclaimed it, and the audiences saw it, told their friends, and came back for more.

Chaplin never liked the film very much. He was involved in directing his own films, and the fourteen weeks spent on *Tillie's Punctured Romance* seemed so much lost time to him. He would rather have his own two-reelers at that moment, than any number of features in which he merely played the actor. In his autobiography he did not even name the film in his text.

Young as he was, Chaplin had a definite feeling in this first year of film-making that his days were numbered. He expected that after four or five years the public would have tired of his variety of comedy. That reasoning buttressed his desire to direct and manage his own work. It also brought about his parting from Keystone. If his artistic life was going to be as short as he expected, then he wanted to milk all the profit from it that was possible. Thus he asked for more money when it came time to talk contract with Sennett.

Sydney Chaplin came to America that year, and he too was hired by Sennett, at a salary even higher than Charles Chaplin's. But not for long. Chaplin was growing restless under the control of Mack Sennett. He wanted more freedom, and particularly he wanted more money. He knew that his comedies were extremely successful by the number of prints that were ordered, sometimes twice as many as for other Keystone films. In the summer of 1914 Sennett offered him $400 a week and the comedian asked for $1,000. The backers in New York were not immediately willing to accept, and Chaplin was getting offers from other sources. What he really wanted was his own company, but he was not quite ready yet for so great a jump. He was saving money; he lived on $75 a week, and saved $100 or more, depending on his bonuses, but he still had only a few thousand dollars in the bank. He signed that year with Essanay Company for $1250 a week plus a bonus of $10,000. Charlie Chaplin was on his way.

In later years Chaplin was to be chided for insensitivity to other people. His parting with Mack Sennett was a case in point; he finished his last Keystone film one Saturday night, spent Sunday in his rooms at the Los Angeles Athletic Club (which Sennett had secured for him) and drove north on Monday to the Essanay lot near San Francisco without a word to his old co-workers. A certain hard-heartedness was indicated. Later Chaplin would say that he did not say good-bye to Sennett because he could not. It was as it had been when he left London and a sleeping Sydney in the next room; the act of parting was too poignant for him.

Essanay got its title from the last names of its two principals, George K. Spoor and G. M. Anderson. Spoor was an
inventor who claimed rights to certain film processes. Anderson was also known as Bronco Billy, and he was the first
of the cowboy motion picture stars. The firm had production
centres at Chicago and at Niles, near San Francisco. Chaplin
went to Niles, did not like it, and decided to go to Chicago.
He liked that even less, for he came in the middle of the
winter, a time when Chicago is always busy living up to its
name as the Windy City. The place was cold in every sense,
including the intellectual, as far as Chaplin was concerned.
He made only one film there, *His New Job*. It was an apt title.
In this atmosphere he also had to work with an entirely new
set of people. He found Ben Turpin in Chicago, and
immediately recognized Turpin's great comic talent, so he
used Turpin in this film and several later ones. Gloria
Swanson appeared as an extra in *His New Job*, and Chaplin
considered her as a leading lady, but she did not want to
become a *comédienne* and she deliberately staged a bad
impression.

Coming raw to Chicago and a much more elaborate
motion-picture studio than Sennett's, Chaplin was struck by
the pretentiousness of the Essanay crowd. That feeling came
over him on his first day, and remained. It was all he needed;
a little shrewd observation and Chaplin had the theme for
his first two-reeler for Essanay, a satire of the motion-picture
business.

In the film the tramp got a job at a movie studio as a prop
man. When the leading man failed to show up on time,
Chaplin was promoted to become an actor. In a huge
uniform, topped by a fur hat, Chaplin struggled through the
part of a leading man, burlesquing actors, actresses, directors
and even prop men. It ended up in a typical Keystone
shambles, but it was more than a Keystone comedy. It had
a point.

Immediately after the film was finished, Chaplin left
Chicago for Niles. There he lived with Bronco Billy Anderson for a time, and tried to put his comedy ideas together.

He laboured under a disadvantage, for at Niles there were very few actors and actresses. In San Francisco he found Edna Purviance, who was not an actress at all, but a pretty young waitress. That was all right with Chaplin, he did not expect her to be able to act, but simply to look beautiful and serve as a prop for his antics and those of Ben Turpin.

Chaplin really had no definite ideas as he set out to make his second film for Essanay. He had a café set, and from there on he was on his own. He knew his own capabilities and some of Turpin's. So he made a comedy very much in the Keystone mould, he and Turpin playing a pair of drunks 'out on the town'.

Three more quick Chaplin comedies came out of the Essanay Niles studio, but they marked little change from the past. Chaplin emerged from the Keystone technique occasionally, as in a dinner-table scene where manners and an overdose of pepper were played to the last laugh, and a scene in which the tramp rolled and lit a cigarette, only to have the tobacco drop out. Slight variations, but much Chaplin.

Quickly enough, Chaplin tired of sharing the inadequate facilities of Niles with Bronco Billy, who made a one-reeler every day. Anderson was just as tired of Chaplin's demands for sets and props, so they agreed that Chaplin would open a studio for Essanay in the Los Angeles area, and he did. Here he made *The Tramp*, the first Chaplin motion picture to open and close a story, even though it was only in two reels. Chaplin was the quintessential tramp, who came upon two other tramps robbing a farmer, and overcame them in a struggle, in which he was shot in the leg. The grateful farmer assigned his daughter to look after the tramp, and the tramp made love to her as he went about his hired man's duties. There was plenty of the old business—such scenes as Chaplin pumping a cow by the tail to make it give milk. The new development was the addition of a pathetic ending. The girl's handsome suitor arrived on the scene, and the tramp saw the end of romance. Sadly, he wrote a little note of farewell, picked up his bundle and walked off up the road toward the horizon. The last scene showed the tramp with his back to the camera trudging along, dispiritedly, then doing a little dance, and marching off across the horizon, ready for the new adventure that life would bring.

A week later Chaplin was doing *By the Sea,* a one-reel sketch improvised at the seashore one day.

Writing, directing, acting, conceiving, Chaplin continued largely in the old Keystone vein. Why not? Those comedies were so successful they were being re-cut and released over again under new titles by Keystone. This summer of 1915 was the year that the Chaplin 'rage' swept America; people were singing about Charlie Chaplin, buying Chaplin dolls, and he found that he was suddenly a celebrity.

Chaplin and his brother Sydney tried to capitalize on the sudden fame, and it was at this time that Sydney began to manage the growing financial complexities that arose from his brother's work. Essanay was immediately more successful in capitalizing on the trend; the company raised the price of Chaplin pictures to the exhibitors. What was wanted was more of the same.

Chaplin provided more. The two-reeler *Work* was a masterpiece of slapstick, built around the troubles of a paperhanger's apprentice on the job. It went through scenes of high and low comedy, and ended with gunshots, explosion, a sea of wallpaper paste spread over all the cast, and Chaplin grinning in triumph at the fadeout.

The difference came partly in subtlety, partly in Chaplin's concentration on the single figure of the tramp. In Keystone days, Mabel Normand was very much an individual actress. Edna Purviance in the new pictures played a rôle that was always subordinate to Chaplin's. Since he 'wrote' and directed the pictures, obviously no one was going to steal the tramp's scenes from him. The result, then, was that the Chaplin films at Essanay built the tramp character more firmly than ever, and as the character came alive, he developed a life of his own, that carried from film to film. His concept of the film story, as opposed to the sketch, was unfolding this year.

The Bank was a case in point, and it involved one of the most complicated plots of the two-reelers. The picture opened with Chaplin entering the bank. After some trouble with the revolving door he made his way to the vault, a spruce and chipper bank manager on his way to work was the indication. But having opened the vault, Chaplin hung up his coat and brought out a bucket, which contained a cloth coat and cap.

Next he picked up a mop, and lo, the bank manager had dissolved into the janitor with delusions of grandeur. Mopping, Chaplin turned the bank offices into a shambles, aided by Billy Armstrong, who played another janitor.

After this slapstick, the plot thickened, which was the new Chaplin way. Chaplin declared his love for the beautiful stenographer. In her office he came upon a parcel: To Charles With Love from Edna. For him, he thought. He rushed off camera and reappeared with an armful of roses which he put on her typewriter. But alas, the present was for a balding young cashier, not for the hero. When the stenographer learned the source of the roses, she threw them in the waste-paper basket, breaking the tramp's heart.

He retrieved the roses, then settled down in his corner, to rest. At closing time, the cashier and the girl went to put the day's money in the vault, only to be set upon by robbers. The little janitor confronted them, defeated them, saved the girl, saved the bank president, and exposed the cashier, who had hidden all this time under the president's desk. Chaplin then, defeated in victory, dropped the flowers on the floor, but the stenographer picked them up, pressed them to her breast, and came to put her head on Chaplin's shoulder, as the police hauled the cashier away. Chaplin turned to kiss his lady love—only then did he awaken from a dream to find himself kissing his mop, while in the background the cashier and stenographer embraced. The poor little janitor got up, kicked the flowers, and walked away deep in his own tragedy.

The little fellow was emerging, a figure of more than one dimension, a man with the soul of a hero inside the pathetic body of a ne'er-do-well.

In this year at Essanay, Chaplin was transcending the boundary of buffoonery, and reaching for high comedy, still keeping the trappings of the past. This was not always so. *Shanghaied*, made next, did not have the poignancy of *The Bank. A Night in the Show*, the following film, was very much modelled on *A Night in an English Music Hall*—with one great difference. Chaplin played two rôles in this film, Pest and Rowdy. Pest was the old music-hall toff of Chaplin's early days. Rowdy was the tramp. Critics said they saw too much of Pest and not enough of Rowdy, of poignancy there was none, but of sudden convolutions of action and plot there was plenty. Here, too, was another development in Chaplin's filming, the use of the unexpected. In *The Bank* at one point Chaplin felt the pulse of a salesman, and asked the man to stick out his tongue. When the salesman did so, Chaplin moistened a postage stamp on the tongue. In *A Night at the Show*, the pest flirted with a girl in the audience, and found himself holding hands with her husband.

The Chaplin reputation in America spread wide in 1915, and it drifted abroad. Essanay raised the rates on the rentals of the comedies. Chaplin soon learned that the company was making a $100,000 or more out of each of his films. He might be getting five per cent of it in salary and bonus. Other performers accepted the property rights as belonging to the company, but Charles Chaplin had none of the preconceived respect for capital that had been engendered into these American actors by their background. He was already thinking like an entrepreneur. So was his brother Sydney.

This year the Chaplin enthusiasm in America became a Chaplin craze. Chaplin dolls appeared in the stores. Other comics were imitating the Chaplin style in vaudeville. On Broadway one show featured a Charlie Chaplin song.

Sydney decided it was time for him to give up his own successful acting career to devote his efforts to managing his brother's affairs. Offers were beginning to come in, the spin-offs of successful public character.

Immediately the best Chaplin could do was secure a $10,000 bonus for each picture, and that was done. But the Chaplin craze continued and increased in intensity. When Chaplin made a trip to New York that year by train, he was greeted by mayors and citizens at Amarillo, Kansas City and Chicago, and when he approached New York the police asked him to get off at 125th Street to avoid the crowd assembling at Grand Central station. It was an era of ticker-tape hysteria in America, and Charlie Chaplin was the darling of the people. But it was not just America. The pathetic figure of the tramp soon transcended western civilization. He gained the name Charlie or Charlot and became a favourite in nooks and crannies of the world that had never seen a derby or a frock coat. Since the films were all silents there was no language barrier. Chaplin projected a universal human image.

Before the year was out, Chaplin had assembled a number of players under the Essanay imprint who would be with him for a long time. He had found his own leading lady, Edna Purviance, the daughter of a Nevada miner, a waitress whom he met at a party. She was young, she was pretty, and she had absolutely no stage experience. She was just right for him, blonde to his darkness, just tall enough and just the proper size to pair with him without looking ridiculous. Chaplin did not care that she knew nothing about acting; he would teach her, and he did.

Ben Turpin also became a Chaplin comedian, along with a dozen others, most of whom vanished from the scene in a few years. Chaplin found a cameraman he liked, Rollie Totheroh, who would stay with him for many years. And they worked hard, Chaplin and his crew, to turn out the Essanay comedies.

For the company, the arrangement with Chaplin turned out to be the most profitable they had ever made. In a year Essanay cleared a million dollars on the Chaplin comedies. Before the year was over, Chaplin had become the single largest figure in the American film industry, and what he did and what he said made headlines in the newspapers.

At the end of that year, Essanay offered Chaplin a half million dollars to sign for another round of film-making. He might have done so had Sydney not cautioned that Charlie look elsewhere first.

Chaplin was coming to the end of his contract when he made *Carmen,* intended to be a two-reel spoof on the opera. Chaplin played the role of Darn Hosiery (Don Jose). The picture was notable for its duelling spoof, also because it turned out to be the dullest picture Chaplin had yet produced.

Before he finished the filming and cutting of *Carmen,* Chaplin was called to New York by Sydney, who had gone there to see what kind of offers for Charles he could stir up in the motion-picture production offices. He had an offer from Mutual of $10,000 a week plus a bonus of $150,000 or about ten times what Chaplin was getting from Essanay.

The contract was signed, Chaplin went back to Los Angeles to work out his Essanay contract by the end of the year. There was really only one more film to be made, and he made it. *Police* it was called, and it was a satire on criminality and reform. The tramp, released from prison, met a reformer who, he was convinced, wanted to 'help' him. Just then they spotted a drunk leaning against a telephone pole, with a watch dangling from his pocket. The reformer stopped close-by to give a temperance lecture to the drunk. When he walked away, the drunk's watch was gone.

There, then, was the end of Chaplin's own work for Essanay. But after he left the company, Essanay decided to take full advantage of all that he had done. *Carmen* was beefed up with out-takes to run four reels instead of the two that Chaplin had planned. *Police* was cut, and a whole sequence taken out of it. A sequence was taken out of *Work*, the unfinished film *Life* was added, and Essanay entitled the three sketches *Triple Trouble*. They also took pieces of *The Tramp, His New Job,* and *A Night Out,* and combined them to make *The Essanay-Chaplin Review of 1916.* And still later Essanay combined a number of old Chaplin films made under their imprint into a seven-reel feature presentation they called *Chase Me Charlie.*

Essanay released these films over a two-year period after Chaplin had left them. The purpose was profits, it was reported that the company capitalized on Chaplin's work thus to the amount of an extra million dollars. The perversion so upset Chaplin, however, that he lost no time in assuming the perpetual control of his later works.

Students were already beginning to find aspects of morality and social commentary in these early Chaplin films. Critic Neil Hurley called Chaplin's little fellow "a pillar of fire in the darkness of industrial society".

Even this early tramp figure represented to Hurley the special Chaplin world:

". . . Charlie symbolized the man on the margin of society,

the man society needed but always overlooked, the 'under-dog', the deraciné. Pretty girls reject Charlie, policemen pursue him, polite society scorns him.

Millions the world over were attracted not only by this gauche character but they felt themselves identified with him. Whatever he undertook to do, he failed.

He tries to enter a subway only to be carried hopelessly along in the opposite direction by the crowd. He tries to open a Murphy bed, only to be imprisoned within it. Even nature offers puckish resistance: the water hose drenches him, the wind carries away the music he plays serenading his lady love.

"But the message throughout all of Chaplin's silent films is one of hope. . . ."

That message was beginning in the early films, but it was not everyone who caught it. Clifford Leech, coming away from a National Film Theatre presentation of 1915 films on the South Bank one Christmas, suddenly realized what he had missed. It was the Chaplin films of 1915 when no one expected the film to mirror real life. In Chaplin's world of that day, for Leech, custard pies were made for throwing. He was a boy, enjoying.

In 1916 Chaplin joined Mutual and began to make two-reel comedies again. From now on he would be reaching for new effects.

Chaplin had one advantage as he opened his Mutual films. Edna Purviance was with him, along with Leo White and John Rand, all people he had worked with in earlier films. Rollie Totheroh, the cameraman he had used at Essanay came with him too. They could, then, swing right into the making of films like those made for Essanay.

All the while he had been making Keystone and Essanay films, Chaplin had been quietly fretting about the pressures that were put on him to produce so rapidly. At Essanay he had cut down his production, in number of titles, but not so much in work. Nearly all the Essanay films were two-reelers, most of the Keystone pictures were single-reel films. With the change to Mutual, Chaplin cut back further on his production. He could do as he pleased for the world was clamouring for Chaplin films. One New York motion-picture house showed nothing but Chaplin films, day after day.

Money piled up for Chaplin that year, because he spent so little. He did buy an automobile, a Locomobile, and he hired a Japanese chauffeur named Kono and a secretary named Tom Harrington. He did not know many people, even though his name was a household word. His shyness kept him from seeking friends and he spent most of his time on the set and off with Edna Purviance. Kono the chauffeur would call for her each day at her hotel and they would drive to the studio.

Since Chaplin would not seek out the world, in 1916 the world began to seek him. Beerbohm Tree came to his studio, so did Mrs William Kissam Vanderbilt, and Paderewski and Leopold Godowski, and Maude Fealy, a famous actress of the legitimate stage. Such brilliance would dazzle anyone, yet Chaplin remained his shy, quiet self. All that he wanted and all that he was went into the work at the film studio.

Others sought him out. He went to see the Nijinsky Ballet when the troupe visited Los Angeles, and when he was discovered in the audience the dancers stopped the show and invited him back stage. They held up the show for half an hour while 'Charlie' visited them. Such acclaim seemed to strengthen his purpose, a remarkable reaction for a twenty-six-year-old young man who had grown up in such degrading circumstances.

The time was 1916. The war was raging in Europe, but America was as yet singularly unaffected by it, except emotionally. With so much bad news in the newspapers and newsreels, the market for comedy had never been better. With Chaplin's international reputation and immense popularity there was no trouble at all in pleasing the public. With so secure a market Chaplin decided he could slow down his production, and take more time with each of his films. He did so, and each of the dozen films produced for Mutual in the next eighteen months would be a complete story, with beginning, middle, and end.

For the first time, outside factors began to have a bearing on Chaplin's art. Early in 1916, when he saw what Essanay had done to his *Carmen* in order to make more money from it, Chaplin became enraged and sued the producers. They countered with a suit for breach of contract, contending that he had not made the stipulated number of films. These difficulties consumed a considerable amount of energy and time. Chaplin did not know that they represented only the beginning of a very difficult period.

The other outside factor was more palatable although it must have been annoying to Chaplin in a way. He secured a number of imitators, including Billy West, who walked off with at least one of the Chaplin players. The most successful of these similar comedians from an artistic point of view was not an imitator at all. Indeed, it was the other way around. In his music-hall days, Chaplin had seen comedies by the French clown Max Linder, who began making pictures for Pathé in 1905. In later years Chaplin was to give credit to Linder as an inspiring factor in his own art. Linder was the 'dude' in high silk hat and immaculate dress clothes. When Chaplin left Essanay that company brought Linder over from Europe to replace him, but the transplantation did not work well, and the French actor soon returned home.

The most outrageous of the imitators was a Mexican clown who had the gall to adopt the name Charles Aplin. It was annoying, if flattering, to see his mannerisms and even his plots stolen by others, but to have his name virtually stolen, too, was more than Chaplin could bear. He finally sued 'Aplin' and secured a judgement that prevented the use of his walk and his traditional costume, the two most salient features of the silent performances. Yet the imitations would continue for the next ten years, as long as the silent films held the stage. This next decade would mark the height of Chaplin's popularity, as well as the height of imitation, and as Chaplin had drawn from Linder and others, so Harold Lloyd drew from Chaplin, as did the Marx brothers.

Several of Chaplin's biographers have adjudged the Mutual comedies to be the finest of Chaplin's art. In them he combined the lessons of comedy he had learned from Sennett with his own developed sense of form, to produce cameos. Slapstick was combined with plot, and the whole leavened by Chaplin's overwhelming sense of the fragility of humankind, where the audience is always left between tears and laughter. The Mutual films represented a stage of Chaplin's development. He could no more have produced them in the beginning, than he would have produced them at the end of his career. When Chaplin began movie-making in 1913 he was twenty-four years old and these films came just three years later, long before any of his major tragedies had come to him.

Chaplin had his problems at Mutual, and the weight of success was one of them. The company built a studio in the winter of 1915-16, and in March it was ready for production. Chaplin had his cast ready, on the company payroll. All he had now to do was produce.

The ideas were slow in coming. Dodgson Bowman tells how Chaplin struggled with ideas, rejecting all that were offered him as too small in scope. As the days passed he began to feel the pressure. The manager of the Mutual lot said nothing to him, but the knowledge that money was flying out the window was a sharp and galling spur. Suddenly, whether it was a visit to a Los Angeles department store, or a recalled visit to a New York store, Chaplin remembered seeing a moving staircase and thinking that it would make a scene for a sketch. In his hour of need he ordered a moving staircase built on the lot, with a department store set around it.

Chaplin played two rôles in this picture. The tramp was the hero, and he was almost the double of a floorwalker who was one of the villains. The film opened with the tramp and his usual comic business. He came into the store, knocking over boxes, squirting himself with the drinking fountain, and falling afoul of the moving staircase, which defeated him. Meanwhile, upstairs, his double, the floorwalker was clouting the store manager over the head and making off with the day's receipts. Soon enough, the floorwalker encountered Chaplin. Puzzled, they danced a little ballet in unison; the tramp raised his arm, so did the floorwalker; the tramp scratched his head, so did the floorwalker. Finally the tramp noticed that the other was carrying a portmanteau instead of a cane.

The floorwalker bribed the tramp to change places with him, and then the chase began. It ended on the moving staircase, going down the Up stairs, and up the Down. In the end, justice triumphed.

The Floorwalker was a slight film, but it was eminently satisfactory to the motion-picture audiences. It was followed by *The Fireman*, in which the tramp character was not a tramp, but a respectably employed fireman. The plot concerned fires, and Chaplin's rivalry with the captain for the affections of Edna Purviance, and much slapstick and derring-do including a Chaplin climb up the face of the building that is somehow reminiscent of Harold Lloyd.

Contemporary writers paid a good deal of attention to these films, although biographers and historians later would place them in the lesser category of Chaplin's works. It depended on what the picture-goer wanted from Chaplin. Certainly in 1916 most of them wanted knee-slapping humour rather than any combination of humor, pathos, and tragedy.

But not all. Robert Payne relates how Chaplin received a letter from one fan who suggested that *The Fireman* represented toadying to "the interests". Chaplin should go back to his irreverent, anarchic ways. He was not ready to go back, but he was ready to change.

In his third film for Mutual, Chaplin undertook a major departure from his own past. Here was the mature Chaplin, appearing for the first time. He played the rôle of the tramp, who had become 'the little fellow'. The film began with him playing on his fiddle and being rejected by a German band, whose members chased him away into the country. He encountered Edna Purviance in a gypsy camp, with a wicked old crone supervising her washing of clothes. Chaplin played for her and stayed with her until the gypsies came to drive the caravan away.

The plot was thickened by the appearance of a middle-aged woman lamenting the loss of her daughter, and it became obvious to the audience that Edna Purviance was the daughter stolen by gypsies. Chaplin found them again, and observed as the beautiful girl was whipped by the gypsy chief. Chaplin then climbed a tree and clubbed the gypsies as they came out of the caravan, stole the caravan, and made off with the girl. For a time their existence was idyllic.

Chaplin washed her hair in a bucket, and they camped out joyously. Then destruction appeared in the form of a handsome young artist who painted the girl's picture and won her heart from the poor tramp.

The portrait won a prize at a fair, the mother recognized a photo of it, and she came in her limousine to take the girl away from Chaplin. As the automobile drove away an unhappy tramp tried to show how cheerful he was, but failed to convince even himself.

That should have been the end of the picture. But Chaplin wanted to go further. The tramp then went to the water to commit suicide, and was rescued by the ugliest woman he had ever seen. With one look he plunged back into the water. This ending came in for considerable criticism at Mutual, and Chaplin changed it: the car returned after Chaplin had said his sad good-byes, picked him up, and he and the girl lived happily ever after.

Experimenting again, Chaplin followed *The Vagabond* with *One A.M.,* which was notable because Chaplin was the sole player. He staged a pantomime for two solid reels, playing the role of the toff in full evening dress who came home, stone sober, to go to bed. The whole was a compendium of misadventures, with a Murphy bed, sliding rugs, revolving table, and a man-eating clock. Chaplin ended up in the bathroom, sleeping in the tub. French critic Louis Delluc called it superb, and devoted more space to that film in his critical appraisal than to any other.

Still, *One A.M.* seemed to frighten Chaplin a little. He was reported to have said that another such performance might be the end of him. Some reviewers (intellectuals) believed it was the finest comedy he had produced, but in his next effort Chaplin was careful to return to the old trappings of his comic art. In *The Count,* Chaplin was again the tramp impersonating Count Broko's secretary. The elements were fakery, a mansion with its expensive furnishings and wealthy guests, silver service for the tramp to steal, antics on the dance floor, and the final arrival of the real Count Broko, the arrest of his impersonator, and the escape of the tramp to fight the world all over again. That was the old Chaplin of Essanay.

The performance might do for the world, but it would not do for Chaplin. In his next film, *The Pawnshop,* he was again experimenting, with irony, pity, and pure fantasy. The finest scene in this film was the one in which Chaplin dissected an alarm clock. Chaplin picked up the alarm clock. He put a stethoscope on it. He contemplated it. He took it apart, piece by piece, until he had the counter strewn with springs, wheels, screws, all examined with the eye of a fine watchmaker. Then, suddenly, he swept them all up and rammed them into the hat of the customer, and got rid of it. His mind was already elsewhere.

There was enough slapstick in the comedy to satisfy an old Chaplin fan completely, most of it involving a running battle with a rival clerk. When Chaplin was fired by the boss for fighting, he invoked the boss's sympathy with his old-tried trick of pleading for his six children. Chaplin enlisted the sympathy of the boss's daughter, Edna Purviance, of course. He made love to her, tried to eat some of her cooking, and in the end as a thief walked out of the shop with the loot, Chaplin effortlessly, felled him with a rolling pin, embraced the girl, and kicked the rival clerk with the back of his shoe, as the scene faded.

The change in Chaplin's style, then, was progression by zigzag. He experimented, tried an idea and then weighed it. He did not again, for example, do a solo performance as he had in *One A.M.*

Chaplin's comic ideas came from everywhere. In the rink he exhibited his athletic grace and skill on roller skates, while saving Edna Purviance from the attentions of a villain and escaping retribution at last by hooking his cane onto the back of an automobile. *Behind the Screen* was a comedy based on the humour of making comedies. *Easy Street* had a very definite social theme that Chaplin had used before: the prevalence of wickedness. Chaplin played a saved derelict who became a policeman, subdued the bully of the block and turned him into a churchgoer and won the heart of the heroine amid a series of pratfalls.

Next came *The Cure,* all pantomime and action. *The Immigrant* was a step along the line of social significance, based on the adventures of displaced persons who arrived in New York. The Charlie figure was developed here; he arrived as a penniless immigrant along with Edna Purviance and her mother, he had adventures in a restaurant when he could not pay for the meal, he ended up with the girl. But the next, and last of the Mutual films was *The Adventurer,* and once again Chaplin retreated to the pure comic. His costumes tell most of the story: striped prison uniform, pyjamas, full-dress suit, and a lampshade that make him a lampost for a moment.

Altogether the dozen films took eighteen months to complete, and the last of them was released in the fall of 1917. Mutual wanted Chaplin back, and offered him a million dollars to stay with them, but he felt that he wanted to be on his own and was willing to make a financial sacrifice to do so. He set up his own studio at La Brea and Sunset Boulevard in Hollywood and went into business for himself. He signed a contract with First National theatres.

The future looked bigger and brighter than ever, but such tremendous success as that achieved by Chaplin in so short a time could not help but have its undertones and reverberations.

The war brought to Charles Chaplin the first indication of the demands made by Anglo-Saxon society on their heroes. Even before the United States entered the war, those who knew that Chaplin was a British citizen sometimes vocally wondered why he was not in uniform. He received some white feathers in the mail. He had threatening letters.

But these were as nothing compared to what happened after America entered the war in 1917. Thousands of letters began to pour in demanding that Chaplin join the service of his adopted country.

Really there was no hope of it. Chaplin was 5ft 4in tall in his stocking feet and weighed about 125lb; the American military services would never have accepted him. But when an examination was held and this was announced, it scarcely stemmed the tide of insult. Chaplin was deeply hurt, how deeply a reader can assess for himself. Biographers have referred to the difficult period, but in his autobiography, Chaplin does not mention it. It is one of the sensitive areas of his life he would prefer to forget.

The only possible answer was to do what he could to further the American war effort without becoming a 'doughboy'. He had made two good friends in recent months, Mary Pickford and Douglas Fairbanks, a pair who were as individualistic as Chaplin himself. Together they put in months touring the country for the Third Liberty Loan. They appeared on the steps of the Sub Treasury building in Wall Street. They went to the White House. Chaplin toured the south, and in New Orleans drew a crowd of 40,000 people. He also made a propaganda short called *The Bond,* with Edna Purviance, and donated it to the government.

With all this success, Chaplin was still a lonely man. Perhaps the loneliness accounted for part of the success; it certainly lent an air of verisimilitude to the loneliness of the little tramp, and that came through perfectly on the screen. Imagine a man whose name was up in lights all over the world being lonely. But he was, and the comedian Nat Goodwin advised him to remain that way. He must stand outside the world if he was not to allow it to encompass him and destroy him.

At First National the change in the Chaplin approach to films was immediate. His next film, *A Dog's Life,* was acclaimed by critics as by far the greatest he had done. French critic Delluc called it "the first complete work of art the cinema has".

It was a three-reel film, which gave Chaplin a little more latitude for expression than in the past. He had perfected his art within the two-reel frame; it was a considerable departure to lengthen the film by half, and it took much more plot and characterization to make it work.

The story dealt with poverty of the kind Chaplin had known as a boy. The little fellow, for it certainly was he in this film, was seen asleep in a vacant lot protected from the wind only by a fence. He awakened, cold, and stuffed a rag into a knothole to keep out the draught. His lot was soon seen as precisely like that of the mongrel that slept nearby beside an ashcan. Charlie tried to steal a hot dog from a vendor on the other side of the fence, was detected by a cop, who tried to catch him but was foiled when Chaplin tied his shoe laces together and walked off with the dog. Dog and man, leading the same life.

Charlie went to the employment office. In a ballet scene there he rushed from one window to the next, always arriving too late, and finally the last window closed on him as he came up. Outside, the dog found bones, only to have other bigger dogs come up and take his bones. The dog's life again.

Dog and man teamed up to assault a cruel society on its own terms. They stole food together. They escaped the police together. At night in a sleazy café, Charlie met the beautiful singer, an innocent country girl. Love and tragedy came next. Chaplin courted the girl, and was kicked out of the café. The girl was fired for no fault of her own. The dog dug up a wallet hidden by thieves and Chaplin came to the restaurant to comfort the girl, found the crooks, who took the wallet. Out went Charlie on his ear again. Finally, after many misadventures, Scraps the dog, Charlie the little fellow, and the beautiful Edna set out to create a life of their own, and the last scene was pure bliss, right down to Scraps' new puppies.

Charles Chaplin next ventured for the first time into open social commentary, with his film *Shoulder Arms,* which was a spoof on the war. Making the film it seemed sensible enough as an idea, but by the time it was completed, Chaplin was receiving barbs for not joining the American Expeditionary Force. Already he had some complaint from England over his failure to fight for the cause of the homeland. *Shoulder Arms* was by far the most effective war weapon he might have devised, even if it was released only a few weeks before the armistice, and then with considerable fear of retribution by all concerned. It was the story of the little man in the allied trenches, his fears, his disasters, his heroics.

The French suffered more disastrously in the war of 1914-18 than any other nation. One would imagine, that if any were to take offence against making comedy of the war, it would be the French, who had lost so many brave sons. Critic Delluc, then, occupies a place more important than most others in his observations. He found it to be a golden work of art. "*Shoulder Arms* doesn't bombard anything and doesn't accuse anybody, but it is much more relentless."

American critics agreed that *Shoulder Arms* did not ser-
monize; from the moment that the little soldier joined the
service it treated his adventures with humour and irony.
Then the dream, in which Charlie arrived in the trenches,
and many scenes of life in the trenches. A bit of propaganda
was introduced, a German officer in the trenches opposite
was shown goose-stepping and kicking his men. That must
have been inevitable. Food packages, letters from home,
guard duty, mud and even lice played their parts in the
picture. In an attack Chaplin captured a line of Germans.
How did he capture them was the question. "I surrounded
them", was the reply. In one scene Chaplin played the part
of a tree in no man's land. In another he was busy bom-
barding the German trenches with limburger cheese. Of
course there was the girl, Edna. Chaplin, and Chaplin's
wooing of her well interrupted when the Germans arrived
and arrested her for aiding an American. In the end, Chaplin
captured the Kaiser, the Crown Prince, and General von
Hindenburg, and brought them all back to the allied lines.

The most severe critics, if there were to be such, should
have been the soldiers. Dodgson Bowman reported that at
the end of the war, a regiment of British troops landed at a
South Coast holiday resort, and were shown this Chaplin
film. "A true picture of a soldier's experiences in France" was
the verdict. Of course *Shoulder Arms* was not that, but it *was*
a representation of the gruelling life and the suffering of
men—and as such it was more telling than anything Chaplin
had done before. "The film justified all that one can expect
from the cinema", said Delluc.

In 1918, Chaplin made an unfortunate marriage to
Mildred Harris, and soon discovered that there were more
unhappy ways of living than with loneliness.

The two films he produced during the year of the marriage
were among the least successful that Chaplin ever did. They
were *Sunnyside* and *A Day's Pleasure* and they were both
heartily panned by the American critics who wanted the old
Chaplin.

Sunnyside was an idyll more than a comedy, exploring the
delights of the countryside and summer. Charlie was there,
a hired man on a farm. The humour involved farm chores,

the herding of the cows, and the catapulting of Charlie on to his head, whence emerged a dream. In the dream Chaplin did to his own art what Walt Disney was later to do to his art in *Fantasia*. Before the little fellow danced girls in Greek tunics. Robert Payne calls him Pan in this sequence, as he joined the dance. The French liked the film, and called it an idyll. The American critics, by and large, did not like the film, and called it a disaster. One even pleaded for Chaplin to bring his comic figure back.

Six months passed after the release of *Sunnyside*. How much did the adverse publicity affect Chaplin's next film, *A Day's Pleasure*? Not enough, said the critics, for him to bring back the clown. For *A Day's Pleasure* was again gentle and almost pastoral, built about the troubles of a family on a day's holiday. There were the usual props and new ones: a Ford auto that stopped at the wrong times, a spilled barrel of tar, a folding chair that kept collapsing, a trip on an excursion boat. But to the lovers of the old rough and tumble Chaplin films of Keystone and Essanay, *A Day's Pleasure* was tame stuff indeed. Even to friends who considered Chaplin to be the consummate artist, the film left much to be desired.

This distaste certainly got through to him. At the time he was undergoing the personal crisis of his first marriage. He was also involved in an artistic crisis, which he later described in his autobiography. Chaplin had discovered with *Shoulder Arms* that he had spent far more than he expected on the film. He had planned it for five reels, and had shot film accordingly. He went to the First National people and asked for an increase in payments for each picture. They turned him down, and reminded him that he still had a half-dozen pictures to deliver. Chaplin offered to buy out his contract. They refused. So he was left with a decision. He could produce "quickies" and fulfil the contract. Or he could assume the cost and do as he wanted to do. Perhaps *Sunnyside* and *A Day's Pleasure* were an attempt to compromise; the bad press certainly must have buttressed Chaplin's own desire to press ahead into the new.

7

The Kid

The war picture *Shoulder Arms* brought Charles Chaplin a new prominence, beyond the mass acceptance he had already achieved with the little fellow and the tramp that preceded him. In this picture he added a new dimension to his comedy. The whole picture was a gentle satire on inhumanity and the folly of war. It left the world with a promise of more to be heard.

In 1919, while he was making *Sunnyside* and *A Day's Pleasure*, Chaplin was planning a motion picture that would far transcend the comic medium. His emotions were on edge; he was in the middle of an unhappy marriage, but his creative processes were operating at full power.

Throughout the Chaplin career one can sense the stimulus and response of his films. With Keystone that was the way they worked: first get the situation, then build a comic sketch around it. Chaplin had adapted the technique already: In *The Floorwalker* he was triggered by seeing a man in trouble on a moving staircase in a department store. But the difference, where Chaplin rose to greatness, was when he began to build character into these situations, as he did in *Shoulder Arms*.

One day Chaplin went down to the Orpheum Theatre in Los Angeles to see a vaudeville show, and during the act of a dancer named Jack Coogan, a little boy came on stage —much as Chaplin had appeared on stage all those years ago in London when his mother fell ill. Chaplin was amused, and obviously the occurrence began to work on his creative processes. He said that it was about a week later that it all began to come together, to use 'the little fellow' and the child in a motion picture. For a time it seemed hopeless, for the news of the rialto was that Jackie Coogan had signed with Fatty Arbuckle to do a film. Chaplin's hopes were dashed. Associates suggested that he find another child; he replied that it would be hard to find another with the quality that Chaplin had recognized in the boy—the indescribable attribute that the film world would christen 'star quality'.

In a few days the word came that it was Jack Coogan the father who had signed with Arbuckle, and Chaplin was quick to make a contract for the boy's services. Chaplin began, then, the production of a film that would tell the story of a boy and a tramp. Immediately he saw that it was going to have to be a feature picture to carry the story he wanted to tell. So *The Kid* was born.

The world owes a debt to London's slums, for had Chaplin come from a middle-class family, he could never have imagined the sheer misery that he was able to suggest in *The Kid*. *The Kid* began with a blast of social commentary on American puritanism. Edna Purviance was shown leaving a charity hospital, baby in her arms, as a nurse stood by with a cynical smile that indicates the woman was no better than she ought to be and would soon be earning her living in the streets. "Her only sin was motherhood" said the subtitle. There the audience was shown that this film was going to be different than anything Chaplin had done before. Even *Shoulder Arms* opened on Chaplin's comic figure, but *The Kid* began with straight drama.

Carl Miller continued the dramatic sequence, playing an artist in his studio, who carelessly knocked a picture of Edna into the fire, where it burned. There in two quick scenes was the whole story of the birth and death of unwed love.

Edna abandoned the child in a limousine, the auto was stolen and the thieves deposited the baby beside a trash bin in an alley.

Of course it was Charlie's trash bin, and the comedy began as Charlie entered the picture for his morning constitutional, debonair as always, swinging his cane and ducking cascades of garbage from the tenements above the alley. He stopped to remove his gloves delicately—the gloves had no fingers. He pulled from his pocket a sardine can, opened it with every nicety, and extracted a cigarette butt. Suddenly he discovered that his gloves had degenerated beneath his dignity, and he flipped them into the trash can. Then he saw the baby in the alley.

The little fellow was obviously torn. He wanted no part of a baby, but his kindliness would not let him simply walk away. He picked up the baby, and deposited it next to another child in a buggy. The mother remonstrated: it was not hers. A cop passed—the little fellow's natural enemy—and Charlie put on his most innocent face. The responsibility more than he could bear, Charlie handed the baby to an old man to hold while he tied his shoe—and ran off to hide. The old man put the baby back in the carriage, the woman reappeared, as did Charlie, and she beat him with an umbrella, and called the cop, who forced the baby back on Chaplin.

Sitting on the kerb the little fellow now faced a decision he could not avoid. Should he toss the baby down the manhole? Glancing down he saw a note Edna had left: "Please love and care for this infant child."

There—a command. Charlie was put on the right track after all.

It was comedy and pathos. The comedy came from the scenes, the pathos from the characters that Chaplin created. The tramp took the baby to his slum garret—Chaplin remembered No. 3 Pownall Terrace only too vividly. Then came a pure comic touch: the baby swung in a homemade hammock with a bottle made from a coffee pot. As the little fellow cut up cloth for diapers, he touched the bottom of the hammock and had to wipe his hand. He then carved a hole in the seat of a chair, put the chair under the hammock and a spittoon under the chair. Chaplin still had not learned about American puritanism. The ladies' clubwomen objected to two scenes in the film: that one above, and another in which Chaplin peeked beneath the baby's blanket to discover its sex.

Having established his film as neither pure slapstick nor pure drama, Chaplin moved ahead five years, and Jackie Coogan entered the picture. The first scene showed him sitting on the kerb manicuring his nails with the same

delicate gesture that the little fellow always used. Like foster
father, like son, said the scene. Soon they set out on their
day's work. The little fellow was now a wandering glazier;
the boy's task was to throw stones through windows and run,
to create work. Jackie threw a stone and broke a window. Up
came Charlie to get the job of fixing it. Jackie reached for
another stone. Just then a cop came up and the boy's hand
brushed the uniform. The camera saw Jackie's double take,
and then he began juggling the stone as if that were what he
had in mind all the time.

Foiled by the suspicious cop, the pair disappeared around
the corner. All day long this went on. The audience was
informed by a subtitle which indicated "Job 13". This time
the little fellow dallied with a lady in the window, and his
enemy the cop nearly collared him. But they had done well
over all. That night in their garret they had a banquet, after
which the boy used a fingerbowl.

Meanwhile Edna Purviance had achieved fame and fortune as an opera singer. When she encountered her own child
in the slums she did not even recognize him. When she
encountered her former lover at a reception they did recognize one another, but there was no reconciliation.

But in the garret life went on as it had for years. The Kid
cooked pancakes; Chaplin arose from a ragged bed in a
makeshift dressing gown—a holey blanket. They said grace,
then attacked their food with the table manners of the slums.

The Kid was found out and taken to an orphan asylum.
The little fellow 'rescued' him and took him to a flop house.
The mother discovered the note she had left so many years
ago, and called the police; the doss-house owner found the
boy and while Charlie was sleeping took him to the police
station.

Sadly, Charlie returned to his slum, to fall asleep on his
doorstep and dream a remarkable dream, in which the slum
was transformed into paradise, with free food and drink—
only to be broken apart by the appearance of 'sin' in the
form of three devils. The dream ended in a fight, a chase,
with a cop shooting down Charlie at the end.

And then, waking, Charlie discovered the cop shaking
him.

Collared, he was taken to an auto, driven to the woman's mansion, and met at the door by Edna and the Kid.

When it was finished, and edited under extreme difficulty, and finally shown, Chaplin was very much concerned about the film. His last two films had been badly greeted. He had been talking to people he respected and many of them had said it was flatly impossible to mix comedy and drama. Well, he had mixed them. He would have to see what the audiences said.

Later he related how he had given a sneak preview to an audience in Salt Lake City, and had waited nervously for the picture goers to react. Then came relief: they began to laugh as the little fellow appeared on the scene with the trash bin, the sardine tin and the fingerless gloves, and they continued to laugh throughout the film.

The Kid could solve financial problems that were distressing Chaplin at that moment, because of his divorce and the heavy cost of maintaining his own studio. Some critics saw in it the elements of *Oliver Twist* and *David Copperfield*. Indeed, the film was wrenched from Chaplin's memories, so why should those elements not be seen? More important to Chaplin, he found that he had been able to do what he wanted to do, to play on life and reality and to combine as life does the slapstick with the tragic. No other film maker had done it thus, and none would ever manage to surpass Chaplin in this phase of the art.

The delicate balance of comedy saved the tragedy from becoming farce; the tragedy of reality saved the slapstick from becoming routine. The secret was that from the outset the audience was made to care what happened to these people—they were people—not the stock one-dimensional figures of the Keystone days.

The last hurdle was the board of directors of First National, who had to be made to pay much more for this film than they expected if Charles Chaplin was to recoup. Faced with possible ruin because of the divorce, and tax obligations, and studio expense, it took a good deal of courage for Chaplin to demand more from them than they had ever paid before. Contemporary estimates said the picture had cost

Chaplin $300,000, and that he got $600,000 from the distributors plus thirty percent of the gross. Later Chaplin said it cost him much more and that he had got more than a million dollars from First National. In any event, the film grossed so much that in the end Chaplin did earn more than a million dollars from *The Kid,* and his financial problems were solved.

8

The Trip

No matter what *The Kid* would do, Chaplin wanted to be free of First National, and he went into production of his next motion picture, *The Idle Class*. Once again he used the double technique: Chaplin himself played the rôle of the rich man and the little fellow.

By Chaplin's own statement, he was determined to rush through the films he owed First National and fulfil the contract as quickly as he could so that he could get on to making films that he considered to be important.

He hurried too fast. *The Idle Class* was scarcely in the film can, when he was setting up at the La Brea studio for *Pay Day*, another 'quickie'.

He came down with the 'flu. He went back to work, disconsolate, not happy with what he was doing, not knowing what he wanted to do. He engaged in one day's shooting at the studio on the new film.

Then, he said, the writer Montague Glass asked Chaplin to dinner. He was busy, he was upset, he was not inclined to accept any social invitations just then.

But it was steak and kidney pie, said Glass.

That was too much for a boy from Kennington Road to resist. Chaplin put down his work and went to the Glass's in Pasadena, where the pie was all his host had promised.

That night, Chaplin was more restless than usual. He had enjoyed himself thoroughly, the Glass's happy marriage was a bright but sharp contrast to his own, just ended. The loneliness came upon him in a surge—and when he got home he opened a cablegram from London. *The Kid* was about to open there, said the distributor. Why did not Chaplin come to help promote the film?

90

The taste of the steak and kidney pie lingered on, and the anticipation of a trip to London beckoned far more than anticipation of more gruelling weeks at the studio. Chaplin read his press cuttings, and he was fully conscious of the impact his films had made throughout the world. He had never enjoyed that success, the shy youth of the music halls had never fully emerged.

Habit was strong. Next morning Chaplin got up as usual, intending to go to the studio. The actors were ready, the cameras were ready. But he did not go. He argued with himself all morning. He showed up at noon, and suddenly made a decision: he would take the trip to Europe, to bask in the sunlight of warm publicity that ought to wash from his heart some of the bitter events of the past year, and to take a rest. That night he and press agent Carl Robinson took the train for New York.

When Hollywood learned that its first hero was leaving town, an unbelievably large crowd gathered to demonstrate at the station. The Press was there in force, demanding to know the reason for Chaplin's departure, when he had just announced work on a new picture. He was evasive, and immediately the Press jumped to the conclusion that he had signed contracts to do films in Europe.

For five years Chaplin had been living with this sort of adulation, and had come to accept it as much as he ever could. His brother Sydney came and so did friends. They shouted and cheered and joined the hundreds of well-wishers who waved the train along as it left the platform.

Three days of rest and they were in Chicago, where Chaplin had a suite at the Blackstone Hotel. Now came a press conference, and the usual barrage of questions, which ranged from

"Why are you going to Europe?"

"What do you do with your old moustaches?"

"Are you a Bolshevik?"

Chaplin fielded them as best he could. He was going to Europe for a vacation. He threw away old moustaches, he said. He was not a Bolshevik. Probably the reporters did not believe any answer.

Chaplin judged a contest. He met crowds. He was mobbed

by photographers who insisted that he produce his moustache, bowler hat, and cane.

He had a moment to see his friend Carl Sandburg. Then
it was crowds and more crowds.

New York was the same. The hero of American folk
comedy did not come travelling this way every day. More
people were interested in Chaplin that summer than in the
President of the United States by far. The photographers
virtually mobbed him at Grand Central Station until he was
rescued by Douglas Fairbanks, who produced a limousine.

They escaped the crowd at the station and drove to the
Ritz Hotel where more people awaited. They made their way
through the crowd at the Ritz, into the elevator, and to
Chaplin's suite.

The Press was lying in wait.

"Mr Chaplin, why are you going to Europe?"

"Mr Chaplin, what do you do with your old moustaches?"

"Mr Chaplin, are you a Bolshevik?"

Charlie answered the questions.

He was going to Europe for a vacation. He threw away his
old moustaches, even after Chicago. No, he was still not a
Bolshevik. He was an artist. He was interested in life.
Bolshevism was a phase of life. He must be interested in it.

Obviously no one believed him.

Doug and Mary, his friends, took him to see a private
viewing of the new Fairbanks picture *The Three Musketeers*.
The Press was again with them. They returned to the hotel.
The Press was there.

"Mr Chaplin, why are you going to Europe?"

"For a vacation."

"Mr Chaplin, what do you do with your old moustaches?"

"I throw them away."

"Mr Chaplin, are you a Bolshevik?"

"No."

That night came a première of *The Three Musketeers*. It was
Doug Fairbanks' night but Chaplin was crushed by the
crowd, mistreated by a cop who did not recognize 'the little
fellow' and a hysterical woman who did recognize him cut a
piece out of his trousers with a pair of scissors.

Next day life slowed a bit. He locked himself up with his

lawyer, Nathan Burkan, but the telephone rang all morning, invitations were delivered, and the mail brought hundreds of letters, most of them asking Charlie to do something for the writers. That night he went to a play, then backstage to see Eva LeGallienne. Next morning he went to lunch at the Coffee House Club with Heywood Broun, Alexander Woollcott, and other celebrities. Another day he lunched with Max Eastman, editor of the radical *The Liberator,* and Eastman asked him to a party. At the party he met "George" an old radical organizer of the International Workers of the World, who was about to go to prison because of his politics. Chaplin was impressed and depressed at once, and very pleased with the crowd because nobody asked him what he did with his old moustaches and nobody asked him if he was a Bolshevik, and nobody tried to cut a hole in his trousers.

Relaxing in New York, waiting for his ship, Chaplin moved easily through the world of the famous. He lunched with a magazine publisher, he dined with Max Eastman and they argued politics. He dined with the Woollcott crowd and posed for a picture by Neysa McMein.

All day long the mail piled in. Reporters showed up constantly, and the telephone rang, with the same old questions.

"Why are you going to Europe?"

Chaplin's temper got the best of him.

"To get away from interviewers", he shouted, and hung up the telephone.

Heading down the pier on the morning of departure, Chaplin was terrified of the American immigration officials. Lawyer Burkan assured him all was well; he had paid his income tax, he had his British passport; the magic of Charlie Chaplin's name would smooth the way. And to Chaplin's intense surprise it did just that. The immigration officials could not have been more pleasant. Then, on board, there was the press again.

"Mr Chaplin, why are you going to Europe?"

Most of the press left the ship before it sailed, but the cameramen did not. As the liner *Olympic* headed for the lower harbour, the cameras trained on Chaplin began to grind and snap.

They came to the Statue of Liberty, and a cameraman asked Chaplin to wave and throw kisses. He refused. The idea of capitalizing on the statue offended Chaplin. He refused again. The cameraman did not like it at all.

The days on board ship passed pleasantly enough. He signed autographs for the children. He tried to exercise in the gymnasium until he gathered a crowd. He went down to second- and third-class to talk to people, but left when he saw a crowd of first-class passengers hanging over the rail to gawk at him. He did not like that. He wanted to be off-camera, he wanted to be Charles Chaplin, and not Charlie, the little fellow, for a while.

He was badgered by people who wanted to know about this film star and that one. He was harried by people who wanted to know how he did his falls. He was pursued by a photographer who insisted he was going to take pictures of Chaplin all the way across the Atlantic. He was asked to appear at the last night's entertainment, and he refused. He tried to explain that the film Charlie depended on props. Some people understood. Some did not.

The ship stopped at Cherbourg. The press came aboard, speaking English and chattering in French which Charles did not understand.

"Why did you come over?"

"Are you a Bolshevik?"

"How would you solve the unemployment problem?"

There, that was a new question. And there were other new questions of vital importance to the world: what did he think of the Irish question? Was he going to be knighted? Would he meet Bernard Shaw? H. G. Wells?

Finally Chaplin escaped, exhausted and bewildered. He slept a little, then as they headed for Southampton the messages began to come in, hundreds of them, invitations, demands, questions—so many that neither Chaplin nor his staff could answer them. And when he did not, the senders were annoyed.

Then came Southampton. Chaplin was greeted by the mayor. Old friends came to say a few words, and a cousin turned up. But the crowds were not there, and suddenly the Chaplin who declared he wanted to get away from it all was worried. Why weren't the crowds there? That was the question.

The ship was a day late, the officials said. The explanation mollified an uneasy Chaplin.

On they went to London by train, Chaplin revelling in the green of the English countryside, and half-forgotten places he had seen so many years ago. Or was it so many? Scarcely eight—but what had happened to Charles Chaplin in those eight years was enough to drive back memories for decades.

At Waterloo the crowd appeared, a jostling, shouting, smiling crowd. He was half mobbed, a young girl seized him and smothered him with kisses. His friends fought the way through the crowd and to the safety of a police cordon. Bobbies came up on all sides and got him into a limousine. In the crush a perfect stranger was also pushed in—in a very English way they introduced themselves, and the stranger got off at the next corner.

It was a king's welcome, there was no doubt about that. The streets were lined with crowds all the way to the Ritz Hotel in Piccadilly. At the hotel the letters and invitations were coming in by the thousands. The Press came, but it was a more restrained press than the American, and Chaplin put them off the first day with a promise to see them the next.

That first afternoon Chaplin sneaked out of the hotel, and alone, found a taxi to drive him around London. He headed for Lambeth, and Westminster Bridge Road. Under the bridge he spotted an old blind man, stopped the driver and turned him back to pause outside the Canterbury. He walked back for a better look. It was the old man he had seen a hundred times before in his boyhood, wearing earmuffs, the same old soiled clothes, the same grey beard, reading from his Bible. To Chaplin he was the personification of the poverty he had known. "It is too terrible", he said and he turned away.

He drove that day past Christ Church and Baxter Hall where he had paid a penny to watch magic lantern slides so many years before. Down Kennington Road he went, glorying in the gentility of its new decay, past the Kennington Baths were he had played hooky, through Brook Street to the upper Bohemian quarter and past Kennington

Cross to Chester Street, recalling the landmarks as he went. He stopped and walked in Chester Street, looking at the children, passing a barber shop where he served briefly as a lather boy. He met a woman who had once been the serving girl in one of his lodging houses, and they spoke for a moment, two people from different worlds with nothing but the past in common.

As he walked a crowd gathered, and remembering the American crowds that seemed bent on dismembering him, he sought the protection of a bobby. But no one leaped on him, no one crowded around him. They stood and looked and blessed him, and then the bobby found a cab, and Charlie was away.

He stopped at Kennington Gate, where he had waited for Hetty Kelly all those days ago. The moment was almost too poignant, for an hour earlier, he had learned that Hetty had been dead for two years. He went to the trolley stop and waited until a car came along to let off its passengers. He looked eagerly. No Hetty. There were no miracles.

He went to Brixton Road and looked up into the rooms where he once had lived. He stopped at "The Horns", the local, and found that it had all changed. Sadly he went back to the hotel.

Chaplin made many little trips around London. Edward Knobloch, a travelling companion and playwright, offered to introduce him to Bernard Shaw. Chaplin got as far as the Adelphi Terrace entrance, then Shaw's house, which overlooked the Embankment. But as Knobloch lifted the knocker, Charlie's courage failed him. If he, Chaplin, was weary of being imposed upon by thousands, was not Shaw even more weary?

He went to a party of actors and the famous on Park Lane, and got into impassioned argument when one toff insulted his beloved Limehouse. He walked home to the Ritz, and met three prostitutes. He much preferred talking to them. How life had changed—or had it? For on the very steps of the Ritz Hotel he encountered a handful of derelicts huddled under the arches for they had nowhere else to go. This was the London he recalled—the cold, hard London of poverty and wealth, the London of the past.

The welcome Chaplin received from England surpassed anything he had ever dreamed about. The letters began coming by the thousands. He was forced to employ half-a-dozen secretaries to reply to them. There were letters from estate agents, from money lenders, from aspiring borrowers, from a barber who offered to shave him, from actors and hopeful actors, from a man who wanted Chaplin to finance a scheme to move windmills, from another who offered to lead him to Captain Kidd's treasure, if he would pay for the expedition. But there were thousands of letters from plain people who simply thanked Charlie for giving them many hours of pleasure—and these were the letters that counted.

Chaplin now began moving among the great and near great. E. V. Lucas, the editor of *Punch* gave a dinner for him at the Garrick Club, and J. M. Barrie came, along with seven or eight others. Afterwards, Chaplin confessed that he had been frightened half to death to meet Barrie.

Soon he was hobnobbing with Bruce Bairnsfeather, the cartoonist, and with H. G. Wells, who again asked if he would not like to meet Shaw. When these and others learned that he did not want crowds, they tried to make sure he did not get crowds. Thomas Burke, the author of *Limehouse Nights,* took him on a walk through Limehouse one evening. He met Wells and they talked about Russia. Chaplin had stored up some future trouble for himself on the ship at Cherbourg, when a reporter had asked him who was most important, Lenin or Lloyd George. "One works while the other plays," Chaplin had quipped—and some reporters put that down in their books for future reference.

In America, Chaplin had learned that it was not proper or healthy to exhibit any admiration for Soviet Russia, and most of the time he managed to keep his opinions to himself. But with Wells he was able to speak his mind, and Wells considered that Socialism would come some day, through the educational process.

As suddenly as Chaplin had decided to go to London, he decided to go to France. He would keep the suite at the Ritz, and keep the secretaries busy with the mail, but he and Carl Robinson would sneak off. Or so they thought. When they reached the station the crowds were there with autograph books and cameras. A few minutes of patience, then they boarded the train, and were off for the south coast.

London to Dover, and then the boat to Calais and for Charlie a rough crossing. But at Calais all was forgiven—the crowds were there calling "Vive le Charlot," until soon he was quite used to the French name for 'the little fellow'. Soon he learned to sign his autographs thus, to respond to the new form of the same old adulation.

At Paris there were the reporters again, even more difficult than usual because the questioning was all in French and Chaplin knew but three or four phrases of French. There he met the famous cartoonist Cami, but they could not speak to one another. He went back to the Folies Bergère, and noted it seemed much shabbier than years ago, just as London seemed so changed. He realized it was himself as well, and the realization made him a little sad.

He lunched with Dudley Field Malone, and Waldo Frank, and the reporters were at him again about moustache, Bolsheviks, and why he was in Europe. He suspected they had cabled New York for their questions, but he answered them anyhow, with what he called his "prop" grin.

There were the funny moments. A personage called on him to ask if he would give a charity showing of a film. He said he would consider it later.

"Ah," said the gentleman, "you are boozy?"

"No, I haven't had a drink for several days."

Dudley Field Malone came to the rescue. 'Busy' was the word.

A young reporter had waited all day to see him, and Chaplin took pity on such patience. But the young reporter could not speak a word of English, and so his exclusive interview came to nothing.

He met Sir Philip Sassoon, then secretary to Lloyd George. He met Lady Astor. From time to time he was caught by crowds on the streets and in shops and restaurants, but the crowds were well behaved and the stay was a pleasant one. They went night-clubbing, and Chaplin drew his hat, his cane, and his boots in the proprietor's book at Le Lapin Agile. He met the dramatist Jacques Copeau. All these meetings had several effects on him. They raised the self-confidence of the one who had been a child of the London slums. They taught him that the great of the world were nearly all easy people, listeners and talkers, and that he need not apologize for his lack of education. But they also redoubled his dedication to self-education; after all when one meets important people, one likes to know who they are and what they have done. All the way across the Atlantic he had toyed with Wells' *Outline of History* and had read nearly none of it. He would read it.

After France, came Germany, by way of Belgium and the Armies of Occupation. He stopped to talk to Americans and British soldiers, and tried to communicate with the Belgians, in spite of the language barrier.

In Germany Chaplin was unknown. He had, after all, come to dominate the silver screen after war began in Europe, and had reached his present dizzy pinnacle just as it ended. It seemed doubtful if the Germans would much care for *Shoulder Arms*.

Those who came to consider Chaplin as a devious radical conspirator would do well to read Chaplin's *My Trip Abroad*, for it tells far better than the autobiography, just how naïve a thinker Chaplin was in the political sphere. He admired Bolshevism; it was as if London's East End slum people had suddenly risen up and equalized their unhappy world. He also understood nearly nothing of the currents and action of European society. Going through Germany, a radical political thinker would have noted that when from the train he saw men, women, and children "working feverishly" in the fields, why children, and why so feverish? It was 1921 and the post-war starvation of Germany continued. That is why. And a thinker would have wondered why the travellers were given a seven-course dinner with wine for about a shilling. Why? Because the frightful inflation had destroyed Germany's financial structure, so would say the thinker. "This is made possible because of the low rate of exchange", said Charlie. Nor did he understand why he did not see much livestock in the fields; he could not equate that shilling dinner and inflation with the absence of animals.

At first Chaplin was virtually unrecognized in Germany. He went to the Adlon Hotel and was turned away. There

were no rooms, said the clerk. Suddenly he was recognized
by the British and Americans in the lobby, and a crowd
began to gather. Karl von Wiegand, the Hearst correspon-
dent, offered Chaplin the use of his office. The Adlon
management soon appeared, spouting apologies and offering
the royal suite.

He and Carl Robinson went to the Scala Theatre, and
were unrecognized. They visited the Scala Café, and no one
paid them any attention. Only at the Palais Heinroth, a
night club, were they noticed and then by Paramount's
Berlin man, Al Kaufman.

No matter what he said, Chaplin was fretting about the
lack of attention he had received from the Germans. The
actor's ego was injured. But now Al Kaufman shouted
"Charlie!"

"Again I come into my own," wrote Chaplin, "then Germans look on, wondering. I have created a sensation at last.
I discover that there is an American jazz band playing in
that place. In the middle of a number they stop playing and
shout:

'Hooray for Charlie Chaplin.' "

All was well. The ego was healed.

That night Chaplin met Pola Negri, then unknown in the
United States although already a famous Polish actress.
Chaplin was always impressed by beautiful women, and Miss
Negri was no exception. He was to see a good deal of her in
Berlin and much more later in America.

Chaplin wanted to visit the Berlin slums, as he had visited
the slums of Paris. Again, here was the social Chaplin bared;
those who wanted to understand his philosophy seldom
seemed to recognize that it stemmed from the same root as
his genius; an immense love and sympathy for the down-
trodden of the world, and a basic hatred of tyranny of all
kinds, economic and political. The trouble with such understanding, in a capitalistic society such as the American
and the British society of the 1920s, was that the public was
never told that *laissez faire* meant economic tyranny, that
unemployment was regarded, as it still was in 1976 by the
American Republican party, as an essential factor in the
economic system. In the 'twenties, few Britons and virtually

no Americans short of the Socialist left even understood the basic weakness of the capitalistic system. Chaplin's gut feeling for the poor would always class him among the 'radicals' in America. He had learned, after a few unfortunate experiences, to keep his social and political views quiet; visiting Acker Street in the Krogel district, Chaplin wanted to "eat with the people" but was afraid to suggest it to his German newspaperman guide.

With the première in Paris of *The Kid,* Chaplin had a taste of the most elegant hospitality France could devise. Paris declared a holiday for the occasion. Most of the ministers of the French cabinet came to the performance, as did princes and princesses and assorted dukes and duchesses, and at the end of the performance Chaplin was decorated, made an *Officier de l'Instruction Publique.* He autographed 250 programmes, made an acceptance speech, and for once was quite overwhelmed.

Back in England, Chaplin spent the last night of his stay with his cousin Aubrey, a publican, and he spent a happy evening in a Bayswater pub. It ended at four o'clock in the morning with a ride back to the hotel in a Ford lorry driven by an impoverished young English aristocrat. They talked, the young man displayed such force of character that Chaplin gained a new impression of at least some of the upper class.

"This is my last night in England. I am glad that it brought this contact with the real nobility."

Next day Chaplin was off, back among the crowds at Waterloo. Old friends and new, and total strangers crowded around to say good-bye. And at the ship there was a marvellous surprise to ease the pain of parting. Hetty Kelly's brother came to see Chaplin off, and gave him a picture of Hetty. Gratefully Chaplin accepted this memento of the woman he would never forget. Then the whistle sounded, and it was time to go. The trip abroad was nearly over.

On the way back to America, Chaplin was quiet and serious. He spent much time in reading, ranging from Frank Harris's racy amours to books on economic theory. Back in New York, one of the first persons he saw was Max Eastman, his radical friend. Through him Chaplin met Claude

McKay, the Jamaican poet, who earned his living as a longshoreman, and they talked about poetry, humour, and the future of the Negro.

Chaplin was showing a sharp interest in social problems. He visited the educator Margaret Naumberg, and investigated her work in progressive education. He took a trip to Sing Sing Prison in upstate New York, and was appalled by man's inhumanity to man. On the way back to Hollywood by train, he noted a newspaper head line, announcing the coming Washington conference on disarmament.

"Does it mean that war will never stride through the world again? Is it a gleam of intelligence coming into the world?"

This was a new Chaplin, a Chaplin aroused, a Chaplin who would quote Tennyson:

> When shall all men's good
> Be each man's rule, and universal peace
> Shine like a shaft of light across the lane,
> And like a layer of beams athwart the sea?

Back in Hollywood it was apparent that the old Chaplin had given way to a new one. How that evolution was to show itself in his motion pictures remained to be seen.

9

Love

This new Chaplin that emerged in the 1920s was the result of a number of experiences. He had gone from pauper to millionaire in a matter of five years, but unlike many who grow rich, Chaplin's money was made so completely through his own genius that his personality remained unchanged. Many in America who begin at the bottom of the economic pile and rise to the top attempt to assume the mantle of the American upper class; usually they go further in parading their opulence and hiding their ignorance.

Charles Chaplin was quite different. Money meant little to him except as a guarantee against poverty, and as a means to pursue his art without compromise. The trip abroad brought back memories, more than that it sharpened the sensibilities of an adult and when he looked upon Europe in 1921 it was with a different eye from the boy who had left England in 1912.

So a social Chaplin was emerging. His philosophy was simple enough, he hated poverty and those who caused it or permitted it. He loved the poor and the unwashed, and he respected those who brought about their emergence, or overturned old systems of oppression.

In Paris, Chaplin had met a café singer named Moussia Sodskay, and had half fallen in love with her. They had argued a little about Bolshevism—she was a stateless person, victim of the revolution—but he had forgiven her all because of her beauty, and tried fruitlessly to get her a visa to the United States. It was his first bitter encounter with the American immigration authorities. Chaplin acted out of love, and he found himself frustrated by politics. That was in a way symbolic. Love was the guerdon of Chaplin's life. How tragic the consequences it would bring to him.

Like many another actor in the world, Charles Chaplin often found himself in love, or at least in love with the concept of love. For love was the antidote to loneliness, and loneliness was the particular bitter-sweetness that had dogged Chaplin since his babyhood. Obviously as a child he was deprived of love. His beautiful, talented mother collapsed from the cares of the world so soon, and his father was hardly more than a bit player in Charles Chaplin's life. Only his brother Sydney was able to maintain a reasonable family relationship with the boy Charles, and at important times Sydney was gone away.

So loneliness was the child's lot, and loneliness was the boy actor's lot, and loneliness was the young man's lot as Chaplin grew up. A park to some was a place to play; a park to Chaplin was a place to wander, lonely.

Early enough he had casual encounters with females, in bordellos and bars, but this was anything but love. His first great love was Hetty Kelly, the young girl he saw only half a dozen times in London. She so captivated him that he continued to dream of her for years, and once he very nearly called at the Gould mansion on Fifth Avenue where she might have been, for her sister had married Frank J. Gould, one of Jay Gould's children. But he did not; something held him back, and eventually the memory of Hetty Kelly was submerged in Chaplin's mind as he became busier and busier in the motion-picture business, and was exposed to other beautiful young women.

One was Mabel Normand. She was Mack Sennett's girl when Chaplin joined Keystone in 1913, but after initial distrust, she and Chaplin got on very well professionally and she exerted considerable influence on his art. But personally nothing ever came of the relationship; perhaps they were too much alike.

In 1915 Chaplin found Edna Purviance, and she became his leading lady at Essanay and his constant companion for several years. In 1915, when he was already a wealthy man, Chaplin was still living in a third-rate hotel in Los Angeles. That year, he moved to the Los Angeles Athletic Club, and shortly afterward bought the seven-passenger Locomobile in which he and Edna rode to the studio every day. Their love affair became common knowledge in Hollywood in those years, but they did not marry, for reasons neither ever explained.

In the beginning life was simple enough, but when Chaplin became nationally, and internationally famous it all changed. With the acclaim came demands on his time, and more on his patience. As Dodgson Bowman put it, a thousand searchlights were focused on him. His history, his habits, and particularly his social life became a centre of attention. Newspapermen and magazine writers wrote about him constantly, and if they did not have the facts, they often invented them.

At first Chaplin welcomed the publicity as helpful in building interest in his films. But by 1916 the interest of the public had far transcended what he considered to be the right of privacy, and it became ever harder for him to put up with the constant intrusions. Soon after, the publicity spotlight became hurtful; others observed his phenomenal success and stole his ideas and his ways. It got so bad that before a film was completed the competitors were in the motion-picture houses with the same idea. He closed the studio to outsiders, he refused to be interviewed except on his films and he began to avoid public places. This attitude infuriated the newspapers and magazines and even as Chaplin's popularity was rising to a peak the forces were at work that would eventually destroy him in America. They would first of all work at him through his undeniable weakness for pretty women.

The first public affair was his with Edna Purviance. They dined together nearly every night after he brought her down to Hollywood when they transferred the Essanay operations there. Chaplin considered marriage, but Edna was very jealous of his attentions to other women, and extremely possessive. When she showed interest in another man, Chaplin's ego was wounded, and in 1916 the romance began to come apart. They continued as close associates; Edna Purviance would remain on the Chaplin payroll all the rest of her life, long after her film career had ended. But there was no more talk of marriage.

For the next few months Chaplin would content himself with work and the development of a great friendship. He, Douglas Fairbanks and Mary Pickford, were the biggest box-office attractions in Hollywood, and it was natural that they would meet. It was not natural that they would become good friends, but since there was no competition between the men, it was possible. They did become the best of friends, and later business associates. It was a friendship that would last all of Fairbanks's life, and be in part transferred to his son Douglas Fairbanks Jr.

But in 1917 Chaplin was again yearning. The vision of beauty and youth that he carried with him persuaded him that year to take up with a fifteen-year-old girl he met at Sam Goldwyn's one day. It was an era in which very young girls aspired to—and became—motion-picture actresses, usually with no other attribute than their beauty and youth. For the most part these were comet careers, they blazed across the Hollywood sky for a few months and then disappeared in a flurry of sparks. Mildred Harris was more than this, she was a stage brat, and she had been acting for several years. She set her cap for the twenty-eight-year-old Chaplin, and she caught him in the oldest way in the world. She announced suddenly that she thought she was pregnant.

Chaplin had lived in puritan America long enough to know something about the *mores*. No public character dare have a breath of scandal breathed about him. Americans insisted that their heroes share the George Washington image.

Chaplin panicked. There was no time to be lost if his error was to be concealed. Within a week he and Mildred Harris were married in a simple, very quiet ceremony. It was 23rd October, 1918, just the time when *Shoulder Arms* was being released. Charlie was at the apex of his career as a comedian.

Was this love? Later Charles Chaplin would say ruefully that it was nothing but sex. They quarrelled about her career, when she signed a contract with Metro-Goldwyn-Mayer. Her 'pregnancy' ended, which was a vast relief, but soon enough she was truly pregnant.

They lived in a big house on De Mille Drive in North Hollywood, but Chaplin, who was making *Sunnyside* and *A*

Day's Pleasure was spending much of his time at the studio, and Mildred was either working or seeing friends of hers alone. Chaplin had known when he married her that she was not an intellectual, it was unlikely that he knew how stubborn and headstrong she could be. She proved that quickly enough.

In the summer of 1919 a baby was born, but it lived only three days. The death of the child seemed to unwind whatever bonds held the couple together, and by the end of the year Chaplin was back living at the Los Angeles Athletic Club.

Chaplin learned to his horror that year just what mischief the fingers of publicity could work in a person's life. Learning that the most prominent figure in the motion-picture industry had moved to his club, reporters began to bedevil him for the story. Chaplin refused to see them or discuss his private life with them. So they began making up their own versions, they began spying, and interviewing any and all persons who had contact with the Chaplins, in the tradition of the reporter who years later was to comb through Secretary of State Kissinger's trash bin for 'important' clues to his way of life.

In 1920, as this scandal was developed by the press, there was certainly legitimate reason for interest in Charles Chaplin, the motion-picture producer. It was estimated that year that his pictures were seen by 300,000,000 people. He would later boast that more people in the world knew the Charlie figure than had ever heard of Jesus Christ. He was far better known than the President of the United States. His appearance at a public function was enough to draw a crowd. If he walked through a hotel lobby, soon that lobby would be jammed with people just hoping for a sight of him.

It was a day of scandal, and that was no help. The motion pictures had grown up so rapidly, without controls, that some producers were violating the *mores* of puritanism every day in film. Hollywood was becoming known as a sin centre by night, the scandals were beginning to mount. In a few months a lurid sex-and-death story would destroy Fatty Arbuckle. Magazines and Sunday papers were thriving on tales of illicit romance, wild parties and orgies. Professionally

Chaplin was beyond reproach. The original tramp was a vulgar fellow, often drunk, sometimes beastly in his temper, and unmannered as a boor. But the Charlie figure that was developing had shed most of the undesirable elements; Chaplin pictures were considered wholesome for the entire family. All the more reason that the reporters should be interested in discovering chinks in the Chaplin armour, particularly when he would not talk about his private affairs.

Chaplin had agreed with Mildred that they would not talk to the Press, but they got to Mildred with an old trick. A reporter called and she told him she had nothing to say. He baited her by saying that Chaplin had blasted her in a statement. She made a strong statement to the effect that he was seeking a divorce. From that moment on Chaplin's private affairs were front-page news in the Press.

Business quickly thrust its ugly head into the Chaplin domestic squabble. Early enough in his relations with First National, Chaplin had discovered that he had made a bad business deal. Working the way he wanted, he was spending so much on the pictures he produced that he was not receiving a fair share of the profits. The acid meeting between Chaplin and the directors had come and gone, and all the good will had washed out of their association. The Chaplin scandal seemed made for the purposes of the First National company.

The press was having its field day. Mildred claimed that Chaplin humiliated her before the servants. It made the front page. She declared that he did not support her properly. Chaplin produced cancelled cheques for $50,000. She said she loved him and did not want a divorce. Back to the front page. She hinted that there was another woman in Chaplin's life. Headlines on the front page.

'Friends' reported to Chaplin that Mildred was sleeping around town, and he tried to catch her at it for this would give him grounds for a divorce that would cost little. He spied on her at the house, and discovered nothing. He spied on her aboard a chartered yacht when she gave a marine party, but the captain of the yacht swore it had been a totally innocent evening, and that at the end of it the men had bedded down in one cabin and the women in another.

Chaplin offered Mildred a settlement reported to be
$100,000. At that moment he might not have been able to
offer more. The building of his own studio, and the venture
into independent production had strained the Chaplin
resources. For a moment Mildred seemed about to accept the
offer. Suddenly she reneged. Chaplin sensed that some outside influence had come into the affair, and soon he discovered that it was his business associates and enemies at
First National.

The plot had thickened in the manner of one of his
Keystone comedies. In August, she filed her own suit for
divorce—which meant she could attack his business assets.
Most important of these was *The Kid*, over which Chaplin
had a new quarrel with First National. The distributors
wanted to release it as three separate comedies, knowing that
they could make more money from them than from one
Chaplin feature. Chaplin stood to lose a good deal of money
on such an arrangement, as well as destroying what he
considered to be a fine work of art.

Suspecting that First National and Mildred had got
together, Chaplin fled one night with the negative to Salt
Lake City in Utah, where the California process servers could
not reach him.

The Press soon learned that Chaplin was in Salt Lake
City, and suggested that he was 'finished' in motion pictures,
because of the comparative failure of *Sunnyside* and *A Day's
Outing*, his last two efforts. There was no time to fight back,
he was busy editing *The Kid*, which was essential to his
financial and artistic salvation.

The charges and statements and mis-statements continued,
but through them Mildred and her lawyers must have seen
the truth: Chaplin's position was more insecure than it had
ever been. If they did not settle there soon might not be
anything to get. The settlement was made out of court,
Mildred's lawyers withdrew the attempt to attach *The Kid*,
which deprived First National of a basic weapon. The
divorce was granted on 19th November 1920.

The marriage to Mildred Harris, the running battle with
First National, the bad reviews he received for *Sunnyside* and

A Day's Pleasure changed Chaplin noticeably. His hair began to grey. He was always moody, but he seemed moodier. Most important, his quarrel with the local press had impressed him so that from this time forward he was cautious and secretive, fighting a losing battle to keep his private life to himself.

At about this time, Charles and Sydney Chaplin brought their mother over from England. Her condition was really no better, her perception of the world was quite unreal. The immigration authorities so noted, and detained her at Ellis Island. More publicity of a private and not very pleasant kind. Finally Mrs Chaplin was installed in a house by the sea at Santa Monica with a nurse, and a hired couple to look after her. Sydney and Charles spent as much time with her as they could, and sometimes Chaplin would screen his pictures for her. She lived on for several years.

After the divorce, the gossip columnists linked Chaplin with a number of young women. May Collins was one. When she left for the New York stage, Claire Windsor came into Chaplin's life. Soon Miss Windsor took advantage of their relationship, and used it for a publicity stunt. She claimed she was kidnapped. The papers were full of the woes of Chaplin's 'fiancée', until the hoax was revealed. It was another wedge in the rift between Chaplin and the Press.

Chaplin and the Press did not endear themselves to one another in the brief affair between the comedian and Clare Sheridan, sculptress and writer. She did a bust of Chaplin, and soon was living in his house. They went on a camping trip with her son. After a week's idyll, Chaplin was spotted by someone, and the Press converged on the scene. They broke camp and scurried back for the cover of Los Angeles, where Chaplin's Press Agent, Carl Robinson, told inquiring reporters that there was no romance. Miss Sheridan, said Robinson, was old enough to be Charlie Chaplin's mother. The Press quoted Chaplin on the front page.

There was an explosion! Next day Miss Sheridan moved from Chaplin's house and Robinson tried to explain to all that he had said this, not Chaplin. Miss Sheridan left for New York.

She was replaced in the newspapers as Chaplin's lady love by Pola Negri. Miss Negri came to Hollywood with a sharply developed sense of publicity. She observed that it was not so long since Claire Windsor had launched a film career, very heavily prompted by her relations with Charlie Chaplin, whom Miss Negri had met in Berlin. Soon Miss Negri let it slip that she and Chaplin were engaged. The Polish actress possessed a temperament as stormy as Chaplin's own, and they quarrelled and made up in the pages of the newspapers, finally to part, in the middle of 1923.

Chaplin's name was then linked with those of several women. Part of the reason was the vast publicity machine that ground endlessly in Hollywood, making 'news' where there was no news, maintaining and feeding the public interest in the most prominent personalities, while the aspirants of Hollywood panted on the sidelines for just such attention. Chaplin was thoroughly sick of the system but there was no way he could avoid it and continue to make pictures in the film capital. He was a primary mark for aspiring young actresses. Once during the Negri interlude a young Mexican girl arrived at Charlie's new mansion in Beverly Hills and somehow got into his bed while he was eating dinner. Naturally the Press had the story. Next day she was found in the middle of the road outside, having poisoned herself. She was rushed to the hospital, her stomach was pumped, and soon she was holding a Press conference at which she readily admitted that she had come to Hollywood not to see Chaplin but to get into the motion pictures.

During this period Chaplin began a long and sporadic affair with Marion Davies, the long-time mistress of William Randolph Hearst the chain newspaper publisher. It was never very serious, Miss Davies knew where her financial interests lay, but in time Hearst at least suspected, and he was not very pleased. He was cordial and friendly to Chaplin for years, but in the end, the Hearst newspapers led the attack on Chaplin that forced him out of the country.

In the early 1920s Chaplin told the Press that he was definitely not interested in getting married. When he built the big house in Beverly Hills near the mansion of Mary Pickford and Douglas Fairbanks, Chaplin built it as a bachelor establishment. When the Press had bedevilled him about marrying Pola Negri, he retorted that he was too poor to marry anybody. *The Kid* of 1920 had been a huge financial success, but the next three movies of the First National contract were quick two-reelers which brought no such return. His studio, his payroll and the new house were obviously a steady drain.

The production of features took an entirely different technique, and it showed quickly enough as Chaplin cut down the number of films. One could not set out with a camera and an idea and produce a motion picture that was to run for an hour and a half or more. A feature film had to be thought out carefully and planned if it was to succeed.

Chaplin had been thinking in these terms for some time, but his marriage and a trip abroad had delayed him in completing his contract with First National. What he wanted to do now was have even more control, and he had established the mechanics when he teamed with Mary Pickford, Douglas Fairbanks and D. W. Griffith to form United Artists Corporation.

Chaplin's first film for United Artists was *A Woman of Paris,* and it was notable for several departures.

Sunnyside and *A Day's Pleasure* had been a prelude to this departure from what had come to be known as the Chaplin technique. Obviously Chaplin did not want to be stereotyped, to continue to produce an endless stream of action comedies. He was growing more mature as a man, and he was developing as an artist.

Seven years earlier Chaplin had begun a serious film which he tentatively called *Life.* It had been discarded in the rush to do more and more comedies. But Chaplin had not forgotten, nor had Edna Purviance, who was desperately eager to become a serious dramatic actress. The romantic attachment between Miss Purviance and Chaplin had never matured, but they continued to be good friends, and she continued to work with him. With his own studio, and plenty of capital of his own, Chaplin could in 1922 do very much as he wished.

The idea for *A Woman of Paris* occurred to Chaplin when

Chaplin with his third wife, Paulette Goddard, and (*below*) his mansion in Beverley Hills

With Winston Churchill

A scene from
Monsieur Verdoux

Chaplin with his fourth wife, Oona O'Neill, and their two daughters, Geraldine and Josephine, in England, 1952

On the same visit, with Chaplin's second son, Sydney, and Geraldine, Michael, Josephine and Victoria

Chaplin in the garden of his house in Vévey, Lake Geneva

Receiving a present from
his daughter Victoria on
his seventieth birthday

With his wife Oona at
home

Geraldine Chaplin in
Cannes for the film festival
in 1967

Michael Chaplin with
Patricia John in Cadaques
shortly before their
marriage

Leaving the Savoy Hotel
on the way to receive his
knighthood, 1975

Aged eighty-five, at home,
still working—
reading a script

he encountered Peggy Hopkins Joyce, a glittering celebrity of the 1920s, notable for her many husbands, her wealth and her famous jewels. She was 'a woman of the world'. He wanted the picture to mirror this 'world'. It was to be a sophisticated tragedy of a triangular love affair. Adolph Menjou played the male lead, Edna Purviance the female, and Carl Miller the second male lead. Production began at the end of 1922 in the new Chaplin studios, and took nine months, with the expenditure of $800,000 and half a million feet of film. Chaplin played in the picture, but so briefly, as a porter, that it took a sharp eye to find him at all.

A Woman of Paris brought the comedy of manners to the screen, and showed the way to other directors. In other words, it was the beginning of a new school of film making, of which Ernst Lubitsch was the principal disciple. He picked up the Chaplin lead and made half a dozen such 'social' tragedies very successfully.

As art *A Woman of Paris* was magnificent. As a commercial venture it was less than satisfactory in America. Chaplin had again violated the American axiom of success: give the public what it wants and what it expects. For years the public had expected to be cast into stitches by the antics of Charlie the clown. That is what the public wanted from Chaplin, not an 'arty' picture. And the public showed, by staying away from *A Woman of Paris*. The film was also attacked by the puritans as immoral because it dealt with unmarried love and pure sex. It was greeted in Europe as a great film, and it helped earn Chaplin a place among the film immortals. But for America it was quickly forgotten.

In the making of *A Woman of Paris,* something else happened that was to be vital to Chaplin's future. Miss Purviance had begun to drink more and stay out later than she ought to do if she wanted to pursue her film career. As Chaplin directed her, he warned that all she did and was showed itself on the film. And at the end, it became apparent that Miss Purviance had lost that girlish charm that Chaplin needed as a foil for his Charlie character.

For his next film, Chaplin decided on at least a partial return to the old comedy style. He would not give up his hopes, there must be something serious and socially useful in it, he believed, but Charlie would be brought back. In Chaplin's life and in his mind comedy and tragedy were totally intertwined, and from the beginning of the United Artists' days his pictures had a message. It was a basic and simple message, that human beings are all caught up by the same forces and that life is a combination of tragedy and comedy, that men and women are the creatures of fate. Part of this change in style must have come from Chaplin's social development; part of it came from the demands of the feature film for a story that can be sustained for an hour or more on film.

Chaplin's new film was *The Gold Rush*, the story of prospectors in the frozen north. He began it in 1924.

Late in 1923, when Chaplin was getting ready to make *The Gold Rush* he began looking around for a new leading lady. He found her in fifteen-year-old Lita Grey. She was small, young, dark and vivacious. Actually, Chaplin had known Lita and her mother for several years and both of them had played bit parts in previous motion pictures. The girl's real name was Lolita McMurry. She read an announcement in the newspapers about the coming film and the search, and applied at the studio for the heroine's role of dancehall girl. Chaplin liked the grown-up Lita Grey, and she sensed right then an animal attraction between them.

It must have been. When the screen test was made, Chaplin's executives did not think much of Lita. She moved badly. She photographed poorly, they said. Chaplin looked at the film over and over again. He listened to his assistants. He made up his own mind and signed her to a contract at $75 a week.

Chaplin began the film with Lita Grey. They shot thousands of feet of film on location at Truckee. They began the dancehall sequences. Chaplin began taking Lita out at night—with a chaperone. It would be good publicity for *The Gold Rush*, he said. They went to premières, to film and dinner parties, to public restaurants where they would be seen and talked about. Chaplin simply could not resist the kind of temptation this beautiful girl offered, and soon he was making love to her. Passion conquered caution, and

Lita's mother caught them one day in a most compromising situation.

Chaplin was in real trouble. It grew much worse when Lita announced that she was pregnant. Chaplin squirmed and fought like a tuna on the hook, but it did no good. Mother McMurray was adamant; he would make an honest woman of her child or there would be the law to pay. It could have been disastrous, even involving criminal charges of contributing to the delinquency of a minor or statutory rape. And there was the matter of time to consider, the number of months before the baby was born. All this was explained to Chaplin by Edwin McMurray, Lita's uncle, who was a lawyer.

Charles Chaplin then faced another unpleasant marriage, made for what were to him all the wrong reasons. The Press had by this time become such a problem to him that he devised an elaborate scheme to throw them off the trail of the wedding party. Through his press office, he announced that he was changing the whole locale of *The Gold Rush* from a Klondike scene to a Mexican scene. That was believable; Chaplin had made such drastic changes in his films before. The location crew set out for Guaymas, Mexico, one November day. At Guaymas, the Press was kept away from the principals, and the technical crew was sent out in a boat to pretend to shoot sea scenes.

Chaplin and Lita drove to Empalme in Sonora and on 24th November 1924, they were married. Lita's mother was there as a witness. To show precisely what he thought of the whole affair and of his new wife, Chaplin left the wedding party and went fishing that day. Lita and her Mama shared the bridal suite.

The subterfuge did not work. A newspaperman had tracked them to Empalme and had the story. Chaplin and Lita returned to Los Angeles, and got off the train secretly at a suburb; even so, their limousine had to charge through a horde of reporters to get into the grounds of the Beverly Hills estate.

The publicity was insidious—it infiltrated everywhere. A few days after their return, Chaplin was beset by the Los Angeles school authorities. Lita was only sixteen, and she had not finished high school. The law said.... So a tutor was hired for the child bride and came every day to fulfil the requirements of the law.

Chaplin tried to adjust, but it was not easy. He and Lita had virtually nothing but a bed in common. Her mother was not much help; soon she was living in the Beverly Hills house on the excuse that Lita was too young to manage the place. The fact was that the bachelor establishment had been managed very successfully for years by Kono, Chaplin's Japanese butler. But the McMurrays would have their way.

Immediately Chaplin replaced Lita in *The Gold Rush* with Georgia Hale, and much of the work had to be done over again.

In all, he spent fourteen months making the film. He said this was the film of all films that he wished to be remembered by. He had said that before, and he would say it again, but obviously he meant it in 1925. The motion picture public agreed and made *The Gold Rush* into one of the big money makers, with earnings of about $2.5 million in America and an equal amount when it was released abroad. Chaplin had given the public what it wanted, "the little fellow" in his derby hat and funny walk, with his constant optimism and his constant disaster until the happy end. There was some critical complaint that Chaplin had slowed down the film and was too serious. But that was the new Chaplin, and he was not going to change. The public found him almost as engaging as before.

As for his personal life, in every way Chaplin's excursion into romance was proving to be the most expensive private venture he had ever undertaken. Chaplin did try to adjust. He took his wife to visit his friends. He took her out in public. They began to share the same bedroom, and it seemed that they might settle down.

The Press was not helpful. Several reporters were certain that Chaplin had been forced into this marriage, and they thought they knew why. One of them came to the house one day and badgered Lita about it. Very soon, then Chaplin moved her out of the house to a small place far from the opulence of Beverly Hills. It was early May 1925—Lita was having labour pains. Soon the baby was born in hiding.

Almost immediately mother-in-law, mother and child were moved to a mountain cabin belonging to the doctor.

Chaplin tried his best to keep the dates out of the newspapers, but was only partly successful. He announced on 28th June that a baby had been born, Charles Spencer Chaplin Jr.

There were quarrels, but Chaplin again tried to adjust to married life with the McMurrays. The next year another boy was born, Sydney Earle Chaplin. But already Chaplin and Lita were wearing on one another. The cultural gap was far too wide to be bridged. One day Chaplin came home to find a party in progress and raged against Lita and her friends. Soon they quarrelled over the bills she ran up. They also quarrelled over Chaplin's affairs with other women. Before the year 1926 was ended, Lita and the children had left the house to live with her grandfather. Uncle Edwin McMurray was brought down from San Francisco to supervise the legal batteries, and the war of divorce began.

As was usual, the Press played one against the other, and soon had Chaplin and Lita exchanging the most bitter barbs through the newspapers' headlines. The divorce complaint amounted to forty-two pages with charges ranging from infidelity to insult and abnormal and indecent sexual acts.

The complaint could not have pleased the press more; Uncle Edwin was out for big game, the McMurrays estimated the Chaplin fortune at $16 million and claimed that $10 million dollars of that was joint property, so under California law Lita ought to have $5 million. The stakes were big enough for Uncle Edwin to move to Los Angeles and join a local law firm that took on the case.

Almost immediately Chaplin began to feel the retribution of puritan America. Women's organizations all across the country began to demand the boycott of Chaplin pictures— not because there was anything wrong with the pictures, but because they must make known their hatred of the man who would not conform. It was the words "unnatural", "abnormal", "perverted", "degenerate" in Uncle Edwin's complaint that really upset the self-appointed defenders of American womanhood.

To escape the Press, Chaplin fled to New York. He might

as well have, the court gave Lita temporary possession of his house anyhow. She claimed she needed $4,000 a month to live in the style to which Chaplin had accustomed her. The court gave her $3,000.

Chaplin was seriously upset by the public reaction; he had never really before understood the American temperament as he was now beginning to do. He collapsed in New York and had to go to bed for a week.

In the east Chaplin fared better than his name was doing in the west, but in June 1927, Uncle Edwin forced the issue. He threatened that unless Chaplin settled the family demands, Lita would name five actresses with whom Chaplin had been intimate. That was the ultimate threat to Chaplin, who could see the danger to his own future, and was not willing to destroy five other careers. He agreed to settle, and Lita got $625,000, and the two boys each received a trust fund of $100,000.

Soon enough Lita's money was going. Uncle Edwin and his friends took $200,000 right off the top. Uncle Edwin had come around one night later to dinner, answered a few legal questions at the table, and submitted another bill for $16,000. Then there was a $90,000 house, and an $80,000 trust fund for Mama, and $20,000 in one season on new clothes, and parties and yacht rentals, and then there were men and there was whisky.

As for Charles Chaplin, the after-effects were so lasting that in his autobiography, nearly forty years later, he devoted one paragraph to his second marriage, and did not even mention Lita's name.

10

Consolidation

The two searing marital experiences affected the life and career of Charles Chaplin in America, and put into animation some of the forces that would later be evoked to destroy him. But in spite of the misery of his marriages in the ten years 1918-1927, other factors were at work to bring Chaplin into full maturity as an artist and a human being. One of these was the capacity for self-education of this London slum boy who had struck it rich.

The Chaplin of the 1920s was a very different man than the boy of 1909 who had gone to Paris with the Karno music-hall troupe, and been introduced to the composer Debussy—and not known who he was.

After 1915, the great and near great sought out Chaplin, and as he met them he learned. He met Paderewski the pianist, Leopold Godowky, who he adjudged better, Nijinsky and the Russian Ballet. He met Sarah Bernhardt, and Sir Herbert Beerbohm Tree, Edith Wharton and Somerset Maugham and a score of other writers, many of them coming to interview him for magazines. He visited the White House and was entertained in Washington in the days before prohibition.

Yet as far as his art was concerned, Chaplin was now ready to enter the period in which he would consolidate all the ideas and techniques he had developed in the past decade. Some critics, Clifford Leech among them, say that all that Chaplin did after 1923 stemmed from the improvisations of the first ten years of film making, and the Karno experience before that. Certainly as far as the public was concerned, Chaplin had achieved his pinnacle with *The Kid*.

He came home from the trip to Europe full of ideas for films he wanted to make. But first he must work off the First National contract—he had no intention of signing with them again for he found them most unsympathetic. The picture business was just that to these men—a business.

The set for *Pay Day* was already erected. The theme represented a Chaplin sobered by his experiences and his voyage. Never again would Charles Chaplin do a simple, almost mindless, picture in the nature of many of the comedies of the past. There is considerable difference in tone between *The Idle Class,* made just before Chaplin went abroad, and *Pay Day,* made on his return. It was not in length—both were two-reelers. It was in treatment of material.

In *Pay Day* the little fellow was a working man on a construction job. The building was fitted with a trick elevator, which carried a good deal of the burden of the comedy, frustrating one player after another. There was no story, for a change. Chaplin became enamoured of Edna Purviance the pretty daughter of the foreman, but Chaplin was married to a shrew (Phyllis Allen). The lunch-hour routine was side-splitting, with the elevator making a cafeteria for Charles of the lunches of the other workers.

It was pay day. Chaplin thought he had been cheated. Actually he had been overpaid. So he put his part of his pay in his hat to keep it from his wife, but lo, she had been following him and she snatched it away. He snatched back, and picked her purse before escaping.

Chaplin then went out to get drunk. Ejected from the saloon, he and three others formed a quartet, and their efforts were greeted with a pitcher of water from above. The little fellow opened his umbrella and kept right on singing.

Then came the confusion of going home. Finally Chaplin found a trolley car, but dozens of others pushed ahead and crowded him out. On the third try he made a flying dive, landed inside, only to be pushed through the car and out the front.

Drunk and disorderly, Chaplin gave up and found another car. This happened to be a hot-dog stand, not a trolley. He grasped a sausage hanging from the ceiling, and looked around. The 'car' was empty. He swayed on the strap, opened his newspaper, and behaved precisely as millions of straphangers behaved in New York, Paris, London, Moscow, and other cities. The proprietor finally disillusioned him, and sent him home afoot.

Eventually the little fellow reached home and his shrew of a wife, who lay in bed waiting, a rolling-pin cuddled at her breast. He oiled his shoes to silence them. He made it to the bedroom, then as he undressed the alarm went off. As his wife stirred Chaplin began dressing—'getting up again for another day'. She was not foiled nor was she amused. Rolling-pin in hand she drove him away, and he sought refuge in the bathroom, and the safety of the bathtub. But the bathtub was full of water . . . .

In delivering *Pay Day* Chaplin was giving First National the last of the comic sketches. He would follow it with one more picture, *The Pilgrim*.

Actually Chaplin owed First National two more pictures, but he was eager to be off on his new career, and persuaded the distributors to accept a four-reeler in the place of two films half the length.

By the time he made *The Pilgrim* in the summer of 1922, Chaplin had felt the sting of American puritanism more than once. Most seriously, as noted, was the hysterical demand for his scalp by various organizations in the wake of the scandal stirred up by Lita Grey's Uncle Edwin and his sensational sex charges against Chaplin. *The Pilgrim* was in a sense the Chaplin answer to such hypocrisy. It was a satire, and sometimes a biting satire, of the world of professional religion. The Pennsylvania censors caught on—they banned the film because it made the ministry look ridiculous. And indeed it did, if one was looking for the ridiculousness of some of American Protestant religion.

In *The Pilgrim* the little fellow escaped from prison, and fortuitously encountered a minister taking a quick swim, with his ministerial garb neatly laid out on the bank. The new 'parson' at the railroad station tried to decide where to go and stuck a pin in the map. On his first try he hit Sing Sing. Finally he settled on Devil's Gulch, which seemed a proper place for a minister. Buying a ticket, he nearly gave himself away by wrapping his fingers around the bars of the agent's cage.

On to the train—where he sat next to a fat policeman who was reading in his paper all about the prison break. Quickly, Charlie got off at the next station to be met by a welcoming committee waiting for its new minister. Misunderstanding, Charlie held out his hands to be cuffed, and the assemblage took this to be a new kind of benediction. A telegram arrived from the real preacher, announcing his delay, but that tense moment passed when the deacon asked Charlie to read the telegram, and Charlie lied that it was about a package, whereupon the deacon tore up the message. Thus was the troublesome matter of the real preacher solved.

Accompanying the new flock, Chaplin went to the church, where he conducted the services, made the collection, and as a sermon pantomimed the tale of David and Goliath. His performance won only the heart of one small boy in the audience. The grim and proper congregation did not seem to be pleased.

Chaplin was taken to Edna Purviance's house, where she lived with her mother. Here he would live, an idea most acceptable to him since he was already making sheep's eyes at Edna. Charlie had to look through the family picture album, he had to endure a visit from a dreadful woman, her hen-pecked husband and their horrible brat of a son. The brat bedevilled Charlie, who took it like a saint until the others left the room—whereupon he kicked the little monster in the belly. The brat had his revenge, substituting a bowler hat for the Christmas pudding. The struggle between them was left in abeyance, because an old cell-mate of the 'parson's' showed up, prepared to rob the house. Charlie had by now become so enamoured of Edna that he took a stand against his old friend the crook, and they fought over the money, Charlie recovering it.

But the sheriff got him finally. Edna would not believe her pure hero was really a crook, and argued for mercy. The softhearted sheriff sent Chaplin across the Mexican border 'to gather flowers'. Chaplin came back. The sheriff booted him across the border, almost into the arms of Mexican bandits who began shooting at him. In the last scene, the 'parson' was shown running along the border, trying to decide whether to jump into fat or fire.

With the completion of *The Pilgrim,* Charles Chaplin seemed to be ready to turn in a new direction. He would make serious films. For years he had promised Edna Purviance that he would make her a dramatic star, and he had not forgotten the promise. For several months he ferreted about in history, looking for a suitable subject. He had always fancied himself as Napoleon—he called the resemblance in their appearance to the attention of friends. Perhaps he would do a life of Bonaparte. Then came his meeting with Peggy Hopkins Joyce and the germ of the idea for *A Woman of Paris.*

This serious drama was far too advanced for the general motion-picture audience. Since it was a story of unmarried love and sex, it earned Chaplin some unneeded criticism from the moralists again. But if it had gone over well at the box office this would be borne. It did not go well in America. Critics and students of the films found it fascinating and ingenious. Small town America did not like it at all. From Chaplin's point of view the film failed because it did not do what he wanted for Edna Purviance. He sent her to Paris, where she made a French film. Chaplin brought her back and employed Josef von Sternberg to direct her in another serious film. It was never released, Edna Purviance went into retirement although she remained on the Chaplin payroll, and Chaplin returned to his own world—the world of creating his own pictures, for his own character.

11

The Pursuit of Art

What was Chaplin up to? That question worried critics, the film industry, and the millions of people who had paid to see his comedies. *The Pilgrim* was released in the winter of 1922-23, to be followed by *A Woman of Paris* which was not funny and in which Chaplin appeared only in a cameo rôle.

So what was he up to?

He was up to *The Gold Rush,* which was to be a feature film in which the little fellow would display all that he had ever learned in his tempestuous film life about human greed, human suffering, and quiet heroism. Chaplin began the film in a happy hour, but before the filming was far along, he had embroiled himself with another child-woman again, been forced into a marriage most unsuitable for him, and was working under the most trying of circumstances. In spite of it or perhaps because of it, he produced a film that all the world loved, from critics to children. On various levels of perception, there was something in *The Gold Rush* for everyone everywhere.

Critic Parker Tyler suggested that Chaplin's trip abroad was the "coronation of the underdog" and if so, then the figure who returned to the screen in *The Gold Rush* was indeed a king. There was something regal about him: who but a king would stroll through the frozen wastes of the north-land in bowler, tight frock coat, baggy pants, big shoes, and twirling a cane? What he was king of was made clear in the opening—a line of prospectors toiling up a long trail preceded the little fellow, who was followed by a large and obviously hungry bear. There, right in the beginning the audience knew that their little fellow was back, and they could settle into their seats for a session of hilarity, and perhaps a tear or two.

The bear followed as the audience enjoyed the delicious sense of danger; then the bear turned off into a cave—he was not after Charlie at all but was just going home to rest. A laugh. Charlie heard rocks falling, he was frightened, he fell down the mountain. Another laugh. He picked himself up, leaned on his cane and it sank in to the handle. Another laugh.

Chaplin headed north through a storm, and was virtually blown into the cabin of Black Larsen, the villain. So was Big Jim McKay, Chaplin's sub-hero. The storm howling, Larsen tried to drive them away with a gun, Larsen was subdued, and then they settled down to starve. Charlie sampled a candle. Larsen left, shot two mounted policemen who had been trailing him, and made off with their sled.

At this point Charlie and Big Jim were so hungry that they cooked up one of Charlie's shoes. It was one of the funniest scenes Chaplin had ever done, the cooking of the shoe, the basting, the tasting, the carving, the eating of the laces twirled about a fork like spaghetti.

As the hunger continued, in Big Jim's mind Charlie was transformed into a chicken, and the audience had a chase, Chicken-Charlie and Big Jim fighting for Charlie's life, until both collapsed. Next morning the struggle began again, and it seemed likely one of them would kill and eat the other (the betting had to be on Big Jim's side) until a bear wandered into the cabin, Charlie seized the rifle and shot the bear. Charlie was last seen sharpening a knife.

Thus hunger disposed of, the pair parted company as the weather cleared, and Big Jim encountered Black Larsen who had jumped his gold claim. Black Larsen knocked Big Jim out, but fate lent its retributory hand, and soon Larsen was finished by an avalanche.

The film cut to a boom-town of wooden shacks and snowy streets where Georgia, the dance-hall girl, had just had her picture taken by a photographer. That night the picture was torn in a struggle with a rude admirer, and the little fellow picked it up off the floor. As he stood in the midst of the crowd, the girl turned and smiled. At first the little fellow was delighted, only to learn that she was smiling at someone behind him. His face fell in tragic disappointment. Yet in a moment he was back to normal, snatching a drink from a waiter's tray, and downing it with relish.

Georgia, the girl, was pursued by an unwanted suitor, she used the little fellow as a foil. She danced with him, but unfortunately his pants began to fall down while dancing. He spotted a rope on a table, made repairs, and then found the rope attached to a large dog on the other end. A cat put an end to the dancing, and nearly to Charlie.

But Georgia still needed Charlie to protect her against the bully's advances. She gave him a rose: the bully attacked him, in the fight Chaplin's bowler was knocked over his eyes, he threw a wild blow which hit a post, and shook down a clock which fell on the bully's head and knocked him out cold. The little fellow strutted out through the admiring crowd.

Soon enough, down the mountain came Big Jim, his memory lost in the blow on the head struck by Black Larsen. He searched for the little fellow as the only one who could help him find his lost gold claim.

Chaplin had been courting Georgia in his inimitable fashion, the girls had treated him as an immense joke, playing tricks on him and pretending to take him seriously. All the while the little fellow knew in his heart that it was just fooling. But Georgia did promise to come to the cabin for New Year's Eve dinner. Chaplin then shovelled snow from one house to another, then on to the next one, to earn money for the dinner.

On New Year's Eve, Chaplin prepared for the party but no one came. He dreamed a delicious dream of Georgia and love, and then awakened to a cold and deserted cabin. He was awakened by shots fired at twelve o'clock, and wandered to the dance-hall, just as Georgia remembered her promise and went to the cabin with the other girls only to see the table all set, and then she suffered pangs of remorse.

Chaplin, meanwhile had gone off to help Big Jim find his claim. They reached the cabin with plenty of food but in another storm. The cabin nearly slid off the mountain, in fact it hung in space for a time, while the pair balanced and scrambled to stay alive. But in the end, just before the cabin fell down the mountain, both were saved, they found the claim, they became rich and bought fur coats and top hats, and they were interviewed by the press on the ship that was taking them home. And so too was Georgia going home, the dance-hall girl travelling steerage. But through fortuitous circumstance, she and Charlie were reunited and in the end the two embraced, obviously to live happily ever after.

It was one of the most successful of Chaplin's films. The critics liked it, although some still complained that the old fast-moving clown had slowed down with the years. The public showed its appreciation by bringing Chaplin a profit of £400,000. That profit stilled the critics within the film industry, who saw the road to failure in Chaplin's method of taking longer to produce each film. *The Gold Rush* was fourteen months in production, and Chaplin shot and reshot scenes as many as twenty times before he was satisfied. D. W. Griffith, the pioneer film producer, noted as the greatest genius in his field, usually shot a scene only once, after endless rehearsal. But Charles Chaplin had his own way—his genius was in taking infinite pains and making sure the final product contained every element he had considered in the creative process, and none that he had discarded. Considering that approach, considering that he wrote the films, directed them, produced them, and acted in them, there was no particular puzzle in the timing factor of these Chaplin films.

For the most part, the films were all Chaplin, and the other figures were stock characters that could be played by almost anyone under Chaplin's direction. Georgia Hale was the dance-hall girl; she was a young and fresh-faced girl and that was all that was necessary. Big Jim, the sub-hero, was probably the most important figure ever to enter a Chaplin motion picture aside from the little fellow. The part was played by Mack Swain, who had worked with Chaplin for years. Swain got only $50 a week for the rôle, and, of course, he shared no part in the proceeds. Chaplin was never noted for overpaying his actors and actresses, for quite rightly he considered them all expendable. People came to see the little fellow and his foils.

During Max Linder's stay in California, Linder had made a study of Chaplin's filming techniques, and he wrote about them for *Le Film,* when he returned to Paris. The secret, said Linder, was in "the method". Linder had visited the studios. He had watched Chaplin rehearse a scene time and again, filming each rehearsal and then screening it to see what was wrong, what must be changed. Where other producers considered the number of feet of negative shot in connection with the final product, Chaplin paid no attention to this expense. Film was expendable. Performance was not. For example, said Linder, he had seen Chaplin making a two-reeler, which ran about 1,800 feet, during the Mutual days. Where the 'early' Chaplin had followed the Keystone tradition and could make a two-reeler in a week or two, the 'middle' Chaplin spent two months on this film. Each scene was rehearsed around fifty times, and shot twenty times, and in the end Chaplin expended 36,000 feet of negative, or just twenty times as much as he would use.

The French, in particular, were interested in Chaplin's techniques, for the French critics, before most in the Anglo-Saxon world, recognized that Chaplin was far more than a simple slapstick clown. So the French magazine *Le Ciné Pour Tous* asked Elsie Codd, a Chaplin secretary, to give them some insight into Chaplin's working day.

It began, she wrote, at nine o'clock in the morning. Chaplin would arrive at the studio. The actors and others would have been there for an hour, the equipment would be in place, the players would be made up and ready, and when Chaplin come on the set in his own costume, he would first inspect his actors for costume and make-up. He would gather the players and technicians around him and then describe the scene that they were shooting, and again go over their rôles.

> Once he has made clear in full detail the subject which is being worked upon, Chaplin makes the actors rehearse their parts, one by one, having previously tried the business himself. Without exaggeration I think I can say that he has played every character in every one of his comedies. The chatterbox of a woman, prattling without pity or reserve, the policeman directing traffic, the ruffian whom one is always waiting to see

come out of the shadow of a door—for all the rôles he first gives the actor his hints, lightly sketched, but certain in its details. Then the actor of the part plays himself, while Charlie accompanies his miming with a continuous commentary of encouragement or criticism, or kindly suggestions. "Just ever so little more vigour in that fling of the arm, Tom .... Yes, that's it. You've got it."

And then, speaking to the player of a villain's part: "I don't want any of the conventional business of the usual cinema traitor. Just get yourself used to the idea that you're a rascal who isn't an out and out bad one, but simply hasn't got any moral sense. Don't put on a savage look. And above all, don't *act*."

In these early movies, before the feature films, there was no script. Chaplin composed the film in his head as he went along, by trial and error. Above all he did not want conventional 'acting', and this seemed to be his most frequent abjuration to his performers.

A shooting day lasted five or six hours as a rule. Chaplin would rehearse, talk, and then unless he was in the scene he would stand behind the camera himself, eye to the viewfinder, before stepping back and telling Rollie Totheroh to go ahead and film. A day might end with one scene finished. And even that might be re-shot later, if Chaplin thought of some new bit of business that would make it more effective.

The next step was taken late at night or early in the morning. Before the other players reached the studio, Chaplin was usually there, in the projection room, looking at all the results of the previous day's work. He would then make notes. The expression on his face on Reel 39 was better than that on Reel 37, but the action on the end of Reel 37 was better than that on Reel 39. So in the final version, Reel 37 and Reel 39 would be cut together.

Chaplin took great care with captions and with titles. Indeed, the film title was one of his chief concerns, and a Chaplin film might go through half a dozen title metamorphoses before it was finished and released.

Then, once the film was shot and cut and titled, Chaplin would take it out to a Los Angeles motion-picture house, without any advertisement, and try it out on a live audience.

"Trying it on the dog", Chaplin called it, and at that point
the film was not yet considered complete. Watching, he
would note if there was some laugh point where there was no
laugh, or an insufficient laugh, or where a new subtitle would
bring out the missing point. And he was always particularly
listening for the laughter of children; if that did not come he
was failing.

And what was the secret of Chaplin's comedy? For Miss
Codd, he spoke up: the secret was no secret at all, but the
application of a few simple truths about human nature.

Now, for example, what I rely on more than anything else is
bringing the public before someone who is in a ridiculous and
embarrassing position.

Thus, the mere fact of a hat being blown away isn't funny in
itself. What is, is to see its owner running after it, with his hair
blown about and his coat tails flying. A man is walking along
the street—that doesn't lend itself to laughter. But placed in a
ridiculous and embarrassing position the human being becomes
a cause of laughter to his fellow creatures. Every comic situation
is based on that. And comic films had immediate success
because most of them showed policemen falling down drain
holes, stumbling into whitewash pails, falling out of carts, and
put to all kinds of botherations. Here are people who stand for
the dignity of power, and often deeply imbued with this idea,
being made ridiculous and getting laughed at, and the sight of
their mishaps makes the public want to laugh twice as much as
if it were only ordinary citizens undergoing the same transfor-
mations.

Funnier even than the Keystone Cop, said Chaplin, was
the person who was pushed into a ludicrous position and
then refused to admit that anything unusual was happening
to him. He gave the example: a drunk is not really very
funny. But a drunk who speaks thickly and staggers a bit,
but pretends that he has not touched a drop is very funny
indeed.

"That is why all my films rest on the idea of getting myself
into awkward situations, so as to give me the chance of being
desperately serious in my attempts to look like a very normal
little gentleman. That is why my chief concern, no matter
how painful the position I get myself into, is always to pick

up my little cane at once, and put my bowler hat straight, and adjust my necktie—even if I've just fallen on my head."

On secret of being *very* funny was economy of gesture. In a way, it was the same technique that Rube Goldberg used so successfully in cartoons on the printed page. In *The Adventurer* Chaplin made one gesture secure two laughs, the second greater than the first. He was sitting on a balcony with a young lady, eating an ice. On the floor below sat a stout matron. While eating the ice, Chaplin dropped a spoonful which fell down his trousers, and then fell from the balcony down the lady's *décolleté*. Chaplin's distress at the ice made one laugh—the greater one came after the audience saw it fall and knew precisely what was going to happen as it slid down.

Deep in Chaplin's miserable childhood lay the basic roots of successful comedy. He knew that people liked to see wealth and luxury in trouble. He had learned that the audience tended to associate with the actors if the actors let them. Thus in the scene of the ice Chaplin played on both emotions: first, the audience laughed sympathetically with poor Charlie when he dropped the cold ice on himself. Second, the audience laughed uproariously when the ice fell on the bosom of the wealthy lady below. If, instead, the woman below had been a ragged scrubwoman, the joke would not have been funny. Probably it would have backfired completely into a burst of sympathy for the mistreated woman.

Of all his 'business' Chaplin regarded as his best development, the use of the cane, which had elaborated so that the stick seemed to have a life of its own. It was forever around someone's neck, or leg, where it ought not to be. The point there was that a walking stick was a sign of putting on airs, and that when the pitiful little fellow came shuffling into the scene in his flat feet and ill-fitting clothing, and pretended to the dignity of a duke, people tended to double up in laughter without further ado.

Chaplin attributed his success in pantomime to his mother. She had a gift for it. Long after she was driven from the theatre by her health, she would stand at the window of the lodgings and watch the neighbours, reproducing for the pleasure of the children everything that was going on, using her eyes, her hands, her feet—all of her. She could see a neighbour coming down the road and tell immediately what had happened to him that morning. One day she saw an acquaintance dragging his feet, and wearing dirty boots. He was walking angrily. He had just rowed with his wife, said Hannah Chaplin, and he had come away without his breakfast. As she said it, the man turned into the baker's shop and came out with a roll.

Chaplin was much affected by such observation, so it is true that his mother deserved the credit. But many a youth forgot such early lessons, and Charles Chaplin never did. Throughout his life he observed people and reactions. Walter Kerr summed it all up in his *The Silent Clowns*: Chaplin was capable of assuming any character that ever existed, and doing so without flaw.

Another aspect of the genius on which Chaplin touched less in his conversations than did some perceptive observers, was his infinite capacity for pains. In the beginning, at Keystone, he was very limited in the pains he could take, and his arguments with Director Lehrman and others were based largely on this difference in view. But as Chaplin progressed in terms of fame and fortune, he gained the opportunity and the luxury of being able to take such pains. In 1914 he made thirty-five films, in 1915 he made fourteen; in 1916 and 1917 he made twelve—or six per year; in the next five years he produced nine films, or fewer than two per year; in 1923 he produced one film; then it was 1925 before the next, which cut it down to a half a film a year, there was one film in 1928, one in 1931, one in 1936; and then they came even more slowly until the end.

Even when a picture was finished, had been screened at a 'sneak preview' before some unsuspecting audience, and was on its way around the world, Chaplin did not stop working. One reason he attended premières of his films was to secure audience reaction. He kept one eye on the film and the other eye and both ears open for the audience. "I notice what makes them laugh and what does not. If, for example, at several performances the public does not laugh at some touch which I meant to be funny, I at once set to work to find what was wrong with the idea or its execution, or perhaps the process of photographing it. And very often I notice a little laugh for some gesture which was not studied, and then I prick up my ears and try to find out why this particular point has made them laugh. In a way, when I go to see one of my films, I am like a tradesman watching what his customers are carrying or buying or doing . . . ."

In Chaplin's search for comic ideas, the broad world was his spectrum. One day he passed a firehouse when the alarm went off, and he saw the firemen through the door, sliding down the pole, leaping into their boots and on to the fire engine, and hurrying to the fire. Immediately Chaplin saw himself in that position, with all the comic furbelows he might arrange. Once in a restaurant, he saw a man smiling at him, and he smiled back. It happened again. He smiled again, but he could not understand why the man kept smiling, until he turned around and saw the pretty girl behind him. He used this scene, most notably in *The Gold Rush* when poor Charlie hopefully imagined that the dance-hall girl was smiling at him.

He took full advantage of the size of the little fellow (his own) and the natural sympathy of the public for the under-dog. Thus his villains were, from the beginning, huge hulking fellows who should be able to destroy the little fellow with one hand. He called it a sense of contrast; he used it in other ways, as in a farm scene when the little fellow walked out into a vast expanse of open field, drilled a hole in the ground with his finger, and planted a single seed.

Then there was surprise. In the music-hall days, Chaplin had learned that surprise was one of the successful elements of comedy. He had, in fact, exhibited this element when he was five years old, in the incident when on the stage he picked up the coppers, thrown to him, before going on with his act, and followed the stage manager off stage to be sure he was not robbed.

In *The Immigrant,* he offered another surprise element. The little fellow was shown on the rail of the ship that was bringing the immigrants to the new land. From his gestures, bobbing of the head, shaking of the shoulders, he seemed to be deathly sea-sick. Suddenly he straightened up, and pulled in a fish on the end of a line. The result was a burst of laughter.

And bursts were what he wanted. One reason for the combination of slapstick and tragedy in Chaplin's art, was his realization long before general acceptance that again contrast was invaluable. A funny scene, coming on top of a pathetic scene, made the funny one hilarious. Two funny scenes back to back would show the law of diminishing returns. What saved the Keystone comedies in the beginning, was the combination of short takes and short films. They were actually at their best in one reel. A feature film, made with the finest comedians in the world, still had to have its moments of contrast. Chaplin had learned that early. Harold Lloyd would learn it soon after, and his motion pictures were carefully plotted. W. C. Fields, Laurel and Hardy, the Marx Brothers—in fact all the great and lasting clowns—at some time or other came up against the problem of sustaining interest and the diminishing returns of constant laughter.

Another aspect of Chaplin's art was his willingness to admit failure and pass on to something else. In the Essanay days, he had begun a film called *Life,* but it was a mixture of comedy and pathos, and as he was filming he sensed that the demand just then was for slapstick comedies, and that he was not going well with his efforts. He had no qualms about abandoning the work, as he abandoned ideas, scenes, and whole films later. But abandoning a piece of material did not mean that he gave up the idea for ever. Nearly everything was stored away in his mind, and at some point he would come back to the abandoned idea and consider it again.

Another important creative factor was that Chaplin was his own sharpest critic. He had around him from the Essanay days onward the usual quota of yes-men, a species that burgeoned with the industry. Many times his assistants would declare themselves satisfied with a scene, and yet Chaplin would throw it out. Sometimes he would hire an actor (or more usually an actress) that his associates found to have little talent. Chaplin saw something in the wrong scenes and the right people that others did not see.

The seat of genius is a lonely one. Chaplin learned when he became employer. Sometimes his employees laughed—

and once he asked them why and they said it was because he had as director made a serious bloomer. They were laughing at the boss, not at the film; had he taken their laughter as indicative, he would have compounded the error. Thus he became famous, even notorious, for asking his associates their opinions, and then paying no attention to them.

This was then the art of Chaplin, and by the time he made *The Gold Rush* he had perfected it. He now said that this picture was the one for which he would most like to be remembered, and as his life turned, so it would be by the general public.

After *The Gold Rush,* for another two and a half years, Chaplin was silent once more. For several months in 1926 he played with ideas, rejecting a number after spending some time examining each of them. This again, was an indication of the pains of genius. All this while he was maintaining the studio, and a nucleus of staff and performers on a payroll. The intuition of the entrepreneur would have put him to work making some sort of films to make use of the overhead; the soul of the artist prevented him from squandering his talent. Some critics say it was inevitable that Chaplin should do a circus film. Given his understanding of the value of the obvious, that is true; the clown's milieu was waiting to be explored by the little fellow, just as W. C. Fields would explore the circus in his own way in *You Can't Cheat An Honest Man.* Larsen E. Whipsnade and the little fellow did so in entirely different ways; Fields was the confidence man, the proprietor of a mangy, bankrupt circus. Chaplin was the little man beset by circumstance, the only major similarity was the glorious independence with which each faced an unfriendly world.

When he began work on *The Circus* Chaplin had lost the services of Georgia Hale because of the long hiatus between pictures. The new leading lady was Merna Kennedy, another of the child-women who were such perfect foils for the little fellow.

As usual Chaplin spared no pains. He spent weeks learning to walk a high wire for a sequence in the picture. He brought in a complete circus with zoo, and he took all the time in the world to get the scenes just as he wanted them to be.

Chaplin's bag of tricks was full in 1926 when he was making this film. He opened symbolically with a star—a paper star in a hoop which a bareback rider on a horse ripped through, disclosing the circus ring. Merna, the equestrian, failed in her trick, and received a cuff and a curse from her stepfather the ringmaster. And as he cursed, the camera showed the circus was failing, the actors were dispirited, the audience almost non-existent.

The little fellow then appeared, standing on the outskirts of a crowd. A pickpocket extracted a wallet from a by-stander, and when the victim protested, the pickpocket stuck the wallet in Charlie's pocket. Charlie then made his way to the hot-dog stand, unknowing. He persuaded a child to give him a bit of a hot dog. But soon he was involved with the pickpocket, and chased by the police, only to escape into the Fun House, where the chase became frantic, then to get into the big top, and become involved with a magician's act.

The audience, seeing this strange figure running about the ring, took the idea that a new clown had appeared, and they clamoured for him. That night, as the tramp cooked a tramp's dinner in a tin can over an open fire, he had new opportunity, a tryout with the circus. Then up came the hungry bareback rider, supper denied her by her stepfather. Charlie shared his meagre meal. This one scene set the two basic Chaplin forces side by side, the slapstick and the pathos.

Next day the little fellow was given a tryout as a clown. He insulted the circus owner, pulled a chair out from under him, ate the apple he was supposed to balance in a William Tell act, and plastered the owner with lather in a barber act. He was thrown out.

But circumstance would have it that Charlie would succeed. During the circus performance he was chased by a donkey into the ring, where his antics again won the plaudits of the crowd. Further antics with Merna as an aerialist kept the crowd laughing even harder.

The little fellow was then hired as a roustabout, with duties that took him all over the circus so that he could play with the magician's tricks, treat a sick horse with disastrous (to him) results and have further encounters with his enemy, the donkey, and other wild life.

Quite by accident, Chaplin learned that he was the hit of the circus, demanded a raise, got it, and began to put on airs. He dressed like a fop, and courted Merna, only to have her fall in love with the tight-rope walker. He decided to become a tightrope walker himself, and soon he was pressed into service in an emergency. Then Charlie did marvellous stunts on the wire, some on purpose, some by accident, until he missed a catch and ended up in a store across the street from the circus.

The wicked stepfather again mistreated Merna, and Chaplin interceded, to be fired one more time. He then helped Merna and the tight-rope walker run away to get married. All three came back to the circus, and Merna and the tight-rope walker insisted that Charlie be rehired, but he demurred, saying three was a crowd, and they moved on, leaving the broken-hearted clown looking after them.

But only for a moment. At the end, as the little fellow watched the elephants and the wagons leave, he crumpled up a piece of tissue paper on which the audience could clearly see a star, and with his juggler's precision tossed it away and kicked it with his heel. So, said the little fellow clearly, went stardom. Then in his characteristic duckwalk, the little fellow moved swiftly toward the horizon, ready for the next adventure of life.

Chaplin by this time had lost some of his popularity in America. He was slow in producing films, and others were producing quickly. The names of Harold Lloyd, Buster Keaton, and W. C. Fields were emerging. Equally important, in America he had violated a primary rule of celebrities. They had no 'private' lives, the press pried at them constantly, and in public they were to show themselves as leaders of public virtue. Chaplin's many love affairs and the scandal that brewed in the newspapers and the film magazines brought him unending criticism as a person, and much bad publicity for his films.

Still, *The Circus* was a successful motion picture at the box office, and earned three times what it cost to make.

In *The Circus* the intellectual critics saw Chaplin marking time. The public liked the film, it was very successful at the box office, but it was not notable for social satire or parody. It was the clown being a clown. Sometimes the narrowness of the film has been attributed to the timing, it was made during the long and bitter altercation between Chaplin and his second wife, Lita Grey, and work was stopped for so long at one point that gossip had it the film would never be finished.

After *The Circus* Chaplin turned back to his childhood for the more serious theme of *City Lights*. Once again he had to find a new leading lady, and for this picture it was Virginia Cherrill, another of the pretty young Hollywood hopefuls that he was forever meeting at parties or on the beach. As was Chaplin's way, he had done some experimental work with the idea earlier, but he had also given consideration to a life of Napoleon and other projects. In other words, there was no simple, clear progression from one film to another.

While *City Lights* was in production, Metro Goldwyn Mayer brought out *The Broadway Melody,* the first successful talking picture. Chaplin was earlier aware of the development of sound track to synchronize with film, but he did not like what he saw, and even when the motion-picture houses began changing their equipment to handle the sound films, he refused to be swayed. He did stop *City Lights* for a time, but he resumed production as a silent film. His rationale was simple and to the point: he knew that he was genius of pantomime, and silent film was the medium of the little fellow. He would never work as a talking character, trying to explain his actions instead of showing them. Besides, Chaplin had another consideration not shared by many Hollywood personalities. His foreign market was as important as the American, and English talk would certainly destroy much of that market.

So *City Lights* went on as a silent film. As for Virginia Cherrill she was not much of an actress, nor did she need to be. She was pretty, and Chaplin could do the rest. As Theodore Huff put it, "all he needed was this girl's physical frame, as a sculptor needs clay of a certain consistency".

He always wanted a type for a leading lady, a sweet young

girl who radiated joy and innocence to be the foil for the
little fellow. Miss Cherrill then turned out to be a playgirl,
who came on to the set with hangovers from time to time.
Chaplin fired her. He nearly hired another unknown sixteen-year-old, then he reconsidered and rehired Virginia
Cherrill. There were other changes. He fired one actor, and
then another. One was discharged because he said he had a
cold and did not want to play a drowning scene just then.
The picture suffered one trouble after another.

Finally it was finished, and Chaplin composed a musical
sound track for the film out of deference to the changes in
audience demand. At the end of 1930 and beginning of 1931
critics speculated on Chaplin and the film. Styles had
changed. The new comedians were the Marx Brothers,
Wheeler and Woolsey, and Eddie Cantor. The Keystone
Cops and the custard pie were definitely submerged. It was
three years since the 'death of the silents'. How would
Chaplin fare?

City Lights opened on a city square at night, then moved
to daytime, and the little fellow was seen asleep beneath the
canopy of a statue as it was unveiled. The tramp escaped
police and the crowd, and then immediately encountered
trouble in the hands of the various types of the city, to slip
through the doors of a limousine in escaping a cop. Thus he
encountered the blind flower girl, who tried to sell 'the
millionaire' a flower. He gave her his last coin and went off.

The girl was then shown in her slum room with her
grandmother. Chaplin, meanwhile had become involved
with a millionaire who wanted to commit suicide. The little
fellow tried to dissuade the drunken man, only to end up
being thrown into the river with a rock attached to a rope
and to him. Sobered, the millionaire invited Chaplin to his
mansion, and they went out on the town. This sequence of
suicide came long before *City Lights*; Chaplin had been
considering the idea for several years; it was a complete aside
to the story at hand. It was made germane next morning
when the millionaire gave Chaplin money to buy the flower
girl's flowers—and Chaplin bought all of them.

Sober, the millionaire did not remember Charlie or the
evening before and spurned him. But drunk again that night

the millionaire embraced Charlie and insisted on giving a party for him, with all its opportunity for Chaplin 'business'. Again next morning, the sober millionaire did not recall his own antics. He awakened with Chaplin in his bed, and ordered the servants to throw the bum out while he packed for a trip to Europe.

Back to the blind girl, the little fellow discovered her in the slum, and heard that she needed an operation. Chaplin then set out to secure it for her, first taking a job, then hired as 'fall-guy' in a fixed boxing bout. But when he entered the ring, he found himself up against a bruiser who appeared to be planning to murder the little fellow. The fight was hilarious, the parody of every boxing bout ever held in the world, ending, naturally, with Chaplin flat on his back and out for the count of ten.

As the little fellow wandered off disconsolately to find the money for the girl somehow he once more encountered the millionaire, drunk again, who insisted that his old pal come home with him. At the mansion, the millionaire gave Chaplin the money for the girl's operation. Just afterward a pair of robbers came on the scene, and after a chase Chaplin was in the hands of the police accused by the butler of robbery. The sobering millionaire had his usual amnesia, he could not remember Chaplin at all.

Chaplin sprang into desperate action, knocked out the lights, seized the money, and made off into the night. He got away, found the girl, gave her the money for the operation, and told her he would have to go away for some time.

Outside, Chaplin was caught by the police, and hurried off to jail. Months went by, the girl had her operation and was cured and came back to run a flower shop. Always she was looking for her wealthy benefactor, the rich man she had first known when he stepped out of the limousine, and who had befriended her so many times, but whom she had never seen. She listened to voices, always hoping, each time she saw a wealthy man. But he never came.

Out of jail, the tramp had never been more desolate. He wandered to the girl's old flower stall. She was gone. He was beset by street urchins, and they created a terrible commotion just outside the expensive flower shop. The girl looked

out, saw what was happening and came out. The little fellow
saw her and was struck dumb. All he could do was look at
her.

"I've made a conquest," she laughed to her assistant. And
she came outside to give the tramp a flower and coin.

The little fellow fled in panic, for this was the moment he
had been hoping for and dreading all these months. She
could see.

She followed him and called him. She stopped and pressed
the money and the flower into his hand. With the touch of
his hand, she recognized him, the tramp—her benefactor.

"You?" she asked.

The tramp nodded. "You can see now?'

She looked at him, her face dulling with the truth. "Yes I
can see now", she said.

And the girl and the tramp stood looking at one another,
the tramp smiling painfully, hoping, but knowing that in the
end there was no hope.

When *City Lights* was complete, Chaplin tried it out in a
sneak preview in Los Angeles. Something went wrong—
whether it was his horoscope, his luck, or bad planning, it
was definitely wrong. The house was only half-full to begin
with, Chaplin said, and *City Lights* was a complete surprise.
Further, talking pictures were in, and *City Lights* was the
furthest thing in the minds of those who had come to the
movie.

Chaplin was appalled by the low key and infrequency of
the laughter. When the preview was over he was sure he had
a failure on his hands. He was also receiving unpleasant
vibrations from Joseph Schenck, head of United Artists.
Distributors had complained that Chaplin wanted too much
for his films, and even though they had made money on *The
Gold Rush* they were resisting the concept of a high price. One
of their main arguments even before they saw *City Lights* was
that it was basically a silent picture. That unusual aspect in
1931 made the exhibitors uneasy.

Suddenly Chaplin, once the king of Hollywood, found
himself being treated like a producer of Class B motion
pictures. He was warned about prices. He was told that no
major New York theatre was available for a première. There

were more ominous signs: a première in Los Angeles seemed successful enough, but the day afterwards the house was unfilled, and the gross kept slipping down, down, down. The critics paid little attention to the film; Chaplin had been off the screen for another two and a half years, a vital period in the development of motion pictures. Meanwhile other comedy stars and comedy teams had been exploiting the talking picture market and had gained followings of their own. Depression had struck the United States.

Most worrisome, and most dangerous was the lack of publicity *City Lights* was receiving. There were many indications that the film would slip into and out of New York City virtually unnoticed—and that was death.

Chaplin was always an artful gambler. As usual he was playing for big stakes, for he had thrown three years' effort into *City Lights* with all that entailed to his production firm. He decided he must again go forth and sell himself, much as he hated crowds and the sort of ostentation that went with motion-picture promotion. Press Agent Carl Robinson arranged for a gala reception in New York, and they were off again on tour.

Joseph Schenck had many reservations about *City Lights*. When Chaplin reached New York, he found the exhibitors had more reservations. Chaplin refused to hedge his bet. He demanded fifty per cent of the gross for the run, and when it was not accepted, he rented his own theatre. Then he raised the admission charge from eight-five cents to a dollar. Remember, it was the depths of the American depression! Chaplin's rationalization was that anyone who would pay eight-five cents to come to see a silent picture in a talking-picture world would also come to pay one dollar.

He was right. The film opened to a big crowd, and by the next day the lines were forming around the theatre and the show was playing to standing room only. *City Lights* netted Chaplin £100,000 in a three-week run in New York alone.

Chaplin saw, however, that he had been gone a long time from the public eye in a period when events were tumbling over one another. His ego also needed some refurbishment after the past few years in Hollywood, where he had ceased to be the No. 1 film idol, and had fallen into a category all by himself. He was, after all, a strange duck for Hollywood. Most of that film capital's citizens could be typed: they were executives in the film 'business' which included producers and publicity men, or they were directors, who might also be or aspire to be producers and thus executives, or they were performers, who were regarded by the executives as something akin to cattle, albeit very expensive cattle, or they were adjunctory—musicians, cameramen and others in the loose category of technicians. Chaplin was all of these. He could not be fitted into a groove, as Hollywood became ever more specialized, and so he remained outside the pale. His personal life had brought him much unhappiness and the hatred of many organizations that purported to police the public morals. He could certainly use a change and a little ego building.

Chaplin arrived in Southampton aboard the *Mauretania* to discover that his troubles had not crossed the Atlantic. Rather, although he was considerably diminished as hero and artist in America in 1931, his reputation in Europe was much greater than it had been before. And Chaplin, ten years older, was ready to capitalize on that reputation where he had not been before. In 1921, Chaplin was uncertain. In 1931 he was settled at least artistically, and not too shy to air his views.

Again there were crowds, beginning at Waterloo. He was not so much afraid of crowds as in the past; he was far more decisive and even rude in his treatment of the Press, which was understandable, if not wise, considering the merry chase the Press had been leading him for a decade. There were obviously many exasperations, but the Press, once aroused, could be a terrible foe, and this Chaplin was learning to his unhappy regret as time went on. No public figure ever won a long running battle with the Press, and Chaplin was to be no exception.

On this trip, the Chaplin party stayed at the Carlton Hotel, and when the Press called, it was some time before Chaplin would submit to a Press conference. The irritation had set in.

Chaplin was adopted by the Clivedon set this trip, and that meant hobnobbing with many of the great of England.

Lady Astor had him to lunch at St James's Square with Bernard Shaw and Lloyd George and other luminaries. John Maynard Keynes talked economics to him, and Shaw talked to him scarcely at all. He became quite friendly with Winston Churchill and the whole Churchill family.

Chaplin had instruction from Lloyd George and Churchill on politics, from Gandhi on the aspirations of the poor of India, and from H. G. Wells and Harold Laski on the anatomy of socialism. His own social and political views were beginning to develop as he educated himself by reading and by his travel; but his views were still quite rudimentary and centred on his own hatred of poverty and all that it meant to the world.

The trip was not all politics and seriousness by far. He dined with the Duke and Duchess of York. He gave a party for two hundred people at the Carlton with Winston Churchill as guest of honour. He got involved with a young actress named Sari Maritza and Robinson had a dreadful time keeping that romance out of the Press.

The Chaplin of 1931 was stubbornly feeling his individuality, and was not inclined to make the concessions to press or others that were expected of celebrities. Chaplin was scheduled to go back to one of his old schools to make a presentation of a film projector to the children. At the appointed hour he was deeply involved in a pleasant luncheon, and refused to leave. Carl Robinson and Kono, the Chaplin butler, had to go in his stead. The children were disappointed and the Press was disapproving. If it was a Robinson publicity stunt, it backfired badly.

Chaplin accepted an invitation to Ramsay MacDonald's for dinner—and failed to keep it. The bad publicity came on like a rash. He escaped then to Berlin for a première of *City Lights*.

In Berlin, Chaplin was greeted with the same near-hysteria that he had found in London on his previous visit. Post-war Germany had discovered the Chaplin films. He was invited to a reception by members of the Reichstag and talked politics with them. He talked politics with Albert Einstein, whom he had met in California. He was most pleased when he found that these important people seemed to take him seriously, not as a clown, but a thinker. He was showing a certain restlessness of genius. He had wealth. He had fame. He had romance in his life, perhaps more than was wise. He yearned for more, and as much as was possible, Europe provided it for him this trip.

He went to France and met Aristide Briand, the premier. He was decorated with the Legion of Honour, this time, not a school teacher's medal. He went to Venice. He went to Vienna. He went to Nice to visit his brother Sydney who had retired there.

Wherever he went he mingled with the great and the notable, the King of the Belgians, the Prince of Wales, and Elsa Maxwell, who tried to collect them all. He was involved in an unpleasant legal matter over the salary of a British secretary which did not help in the publicity department. He was commanded to a benefit vaudeville performance in London by the King, and he sent a cash contribution instead. The publicity result of that *faux pas* exploded like a bomb across England. In Rome he met Mussolini too, and was not well impressed because Il Duce had little time for the clown.

Always there were young women, and even Carl Robinson could not keep all their names out of the press. May Reeves became a celebrity almost entirely on the basis of her association with Chaplin on the continent, and subsequently published a romantic memoir about her intimacy with Chaplin. The romance had been quite serious and Chaplin had considered taking Miss Reeves back to America. It collapsed for the same reason other Chaplin romances had failed. Miss Reeves made the error of dallying momentarily with another. Chaplin would not play second fiddle to anyone and he would not forgive.

The European tour became a world tour. Chaplin went to Ceylon and Malaya, to the East Indies, and finally arrived in Japan in the spring of 1932. Again he received the royal welcome. In Japan, Chaplin showed considerable interest in Japanese drama. He also went through the round of entertainments. The Japanese trip was notable because he was very nearly assassinated, and one of his hosts, Premier Inukai, was killed by the Black Dragon Society which was undertaking the militarization of Japan by assassination and terror. Chaplin's crime was that he represented American capitalism!

Japan was the last foreign stop on the trip. Then it was back to America. Already he had an idea for a new motion picture.

12

The Social Rôle

The great depression, acting as an enzyme on his miserable childhood, brought forth in Charles Chaplin in the 1930s a serious concern with the direction of Western society. On his first trip abroad Chaplin had been content with lionization and his conversation dealt largely with the arts of the cinema. Ten years later he eagerly pursued political and economic matters, and as he was exposed to ideas he developed a social philosophy.

Westerners, and Americans in particular, have never been very keen on the mixture of art and politics. They liked their clowns to be clowns and not budding politicians or economic seers. Sometimes art and politics approached one another, but not often. Ronald Reagan, the actor of the 1930s and 1940s became a politician in the 1960s, but his film career was behind him. Other film actors sometimes entered the political scene, but usually as supporting players, lending whatever personal following they had to the cause of the party and person they espoused. Never has it been a very happy mixture, and American politicians have always been wary of the Hollywood vote.

Charles Chaplin's entry into the political arena was gradual and not overly obtrusive. He liked to talk to other prominent people about his ideas. He spent hours with H. G. Wells talking socialism, but his interests were really more basic and economic than political. He was a Populist who believed in easy credit and expansion of the money supply to resolve the problems of world depression. On his return from the tour, he wrote several articles for the press on currency reform. He believed philosophically in socialism. He considered himself an international figure—which he was—and a citizen of the world, which was a little more complicated. His social views were sometimes inconsistent: at one point in Europe he had argued against modern machinery, only to argue for modern machinery as the solution to India's economic problems. But then Gandhi had suggested that India's economic problems could not be solved until her political problems were resolved and she was free of Britain. It was, as Chaplin learned on the tour, a very complicated world.

His new motion picture, *Modern Times* was to have definite political overtones. He could not avoid that unless he changed the subject, for a picture satirizing the assembly line, and industrial practices and urban misery in the depression of the 1930s was bound to be regarded politically.

Not only the nation, but the motion-picture industry had changed sharply in the past few years. Chaplin, the silent clown, found himself a lonely anomaly in a sound-struck Hollywood. The new medium had brought more than an addition to pictures, it had changed the tempo, slowed it down and made pictures not only talking but talky, as it destroyed more than half the body-motion that had made pictures such a universal medium in the past. Simplicity was lost, and with it much of the beauty too. The little fellow could never survive the 'talkies', yet he was to have one more outing as Chaplin sought his own compromise with modern times.

Genius is never secure, and Chaplin was not secure in his art in a changing world. As he reported in his autobiography, he was often stricken by the remarks of critics. At about this time, one critic accused him of sentimentality in his film making, and said that Chaplin must attempt to approximate realism. There, of course, was the road to politicization; he had already been given large doses of political and economic theory on his trip abroad, and he was well aware that Bernard Shaw believed thoroughly in the use of art for propaganda. He had argued that point in the past; the opposite argument was having its effects on him, for like every other resident of the United States, Chaplin could not help but be affected by the depression he saw everywhere around him. If one had to measure the factors that brought about the politicization of Charles Chaplin, one could certainly say that the most important single factor was the sudden descent of poverty on America in 1930. Not that there had not been poverty in America before, but American society claimed an upward mobility, and that mobility was brought screechingly to a halt. The Russians, Shaw, Wells, and others that Chaplin respected had long been predicting the collapse of capitalism under its own dead weight. In 1931 and 1932 it certainly seemed that capitalism was tottering. The stoutest defenders of *laissez faire* were more than usually nervous, and looked with suspicion on any criticism of the system that had failed, to be rescued by Franklin D. Roosevelt with borrowings from socialist theory. Thus as Charles Chaplin considered a motion picture dealing with the industrial society, he was putting his head in a noose. How little he understood was indicated in his working title for the film—*The Masses*. Such a title, from what had become Bolshevik jargon, might have been fatal in America. Before the end, Chaplin was persuaded to change the title.

Modern Times had a new leading lady. Chaplin said that his most vulnerable period as far as women were concerned was that time when he had finished a picture and had not yet started another. At leisure, the highly-sexed actor was constantly involved with women. He came home from the eight-months world tour without a lover, since he had jettisoned May Reeves in Europe, and almost immediately he met Paulette Goddard, a young actress who was making a picture for Samuel Goldwyn. Paulette Goddard had just ended an unhappy marriage, and she was as much at a loose end as Chaplin. They met one weekend aboard Joseph Schenck's yacht and immediately became what the libel-conscious Hollywood gossip columnists euphemistically termed "inseparable companions".

Modern Times was conceived and made with the same slow care that Chaplin had invoked in his last two motion pictures. Filming began in the autumn of 1934, but for two years he had worked on the script, and made preparations. Miss Goddard was already an actress, but Chaplin engaged teachers to sharpen her singing and improve her dancing. He visited factories to see assembly lines and finally constructed on his own lot a working assembly line of wood and rubber (painted black) which actually worked.

Sound, once again, was to be used as an effect. Chaplin wrote a score for the picture, and used certain noises. There were even voices heard, but they were inhuman, they came from a loud speaker and their purpose was noise. *Modern Times* was to be a silent movie, running firmly against the tide.

Modern Times was a satire on industrialization and the inhumanity of the factory system. It was funny and it was meant to be funny. But Chaplin had fully matured as a personality and he now showed how much he had been affected by the times and the philosophies he had been hearing from those awesome figures among whom he moved abroad, as played against his own child-bred consciousness of misery. Robert Payne calls it "an essay in the agony of our time". It was precisely that.

The public was waiting for social commentary from Chaplin. The word was out in the industry that he was going to blow the lid off. His public remarks in the past few years, and particularly on the world journey, indicated that Chaplin had become a political creature, at least a socialist, if not worse, by capitalist standards.

Yet when the film was released in February, 1936, once again Charlie Chaplin had produced a comedy—one with sober and sometimes frightening overtones. One reason the overtones were given so much attention was the change in modern society. One could go back to *Shoulder Arms* and talk about message and propaganda, although in 1918 and 1919 few people did. The society of the 1930s was a more sombre world society than that of the past, and Chaplin's efforts must be considered within that context.

Modern Times opened on sheep rushing through a farm gate and switched immediately to factory workers running to work. The little fellow was one of them. His job on the assembly line was to tighten bolts with two monkey wrenches. The audience did not know what he was making, he did not know what he was making, Chaplin the producer did not know what he was making. That was unimportant. He was tightening two bolts on an endless conveyor belt, second after second, minute after minute, hour after hour, day after day, month after month, year after year. It was all right there: the concept of industrial misery.

Inevitably, because this was a film about the little fellow, he became enmeshed in the machinery, clogging up production and the assembly line, in an hilarious fashion reminiscent of scenes from a funhouse.

Charlie moved on to explore other aspects of mass production. The boss, driving for efficiency, decided to cut the waste time of lunch hour by introducing a feeding machine. Charlie was the guinea pig. He was seated in the contraption and force-fed. Spoons came at him, a machine delivered and turned an ear of corn against his teeth. But the machine broke down, and Charlie was fed nuts and bolts and drowned in soup and plastered with pie—trapped in the infernal machine.

This tortured life of the assembly line drove Charlie to a nervous breakdown and he was sent to the loony bin. Recovered, he found he had no job and joined the long line of the unemployed. Finally he got a job, only to have a strike called immediately. The cops came, and as they always did in every Chaplin movie, they picked on Charlie. He stole a ride on a truck, fell off and picked up the red flag on the end to wave to the driver to attract his attention. While he was waving, he was overtaken by a communist demonstration. There was Charlie, red flag in hand, as the communists came up and surged about him. Down swooped the cops; there was the red leader with the red flag, *in flagrante delicto*—and off went Charlie just like old times to goal; poor, innocent, *gaol.* misunderstood Charlie.

In prison, Charlie adjusted rapidly as he always adjusted, and soon he had a comfortable cell. Just then, of course, he was pardoned and thrown back into the cruel world of industry.

Charlie found a job in a shipyard, where he launched and sank an unfinished ship, and was fired again. He then met Paulette Goddard, a ragged street urchin who was on the run from the police for shoplifting food for her starving sisters. The police caught her; smitten Charlie tried to take the blame but she was dragged off in a paddy wagon.

Charlie wanted to get arrested. He went to a restaurant, ordered a huge meal, and then announced he had no money. He was arrested, he was put in the same paddy wagon with the girl, and they escaped together, to find a hut on the waterfront, and settled down to a happy life of misery, Charlie sleeping in the doghouse outside the hut for propriety's sake.

The little fellow got a job as watchman in a department store, and he and the girl cavorted there, she in an ermine coat from a mannequin. But the store was invaded by amateur robbers, unemployed workers from the factory, and the little fellow recognized and helped them. Again the cops came, and Chaplin went to jail once more.

Her protector in jail, the girl got a job in a cabaret, and when he came out she got him a job as a waiter. They dreamed together of a suburban cottage—the American ideal promoted by the ladies' magazines. But the little fellow was a terrible waiter. In trouble, he was saved when the male singer failed to show for his act. Charlie substituted for him, made a hit, and all looked bright—until the cops came again, this time the juvenile officers coming to arrest Miss Goddard as an underage delinquent. This odd development may have had root in Chaplin's private life. It was not many years before that Lita Grey had been hauled before the juvenile authorities and forced to go to school because she was only sixteen years old—even though she was married to Chaplin and matron of his mansion.

They escaped. Like the rest of the world, their bad luck dropped them into depression. But they saw they had one another, and they linked arms and walked off, as the little fellow had done alone so many times before, into the horizon.

Critics usually find what they seek in any production. The critics of the right saw in Chaplin's movie the sinister arm of communism. A time of trouble, they indicated, was no time in which any right-thinking person would criticize the industrial society. Chambers of Commerce and industrial trade organizations were furious, and the least insulting name they had for Chaplin was 'parlor pink'.

One problem was that critics in America were looking for

social significance, and they saw more in the conveyor belt scenes, the red flag waving, the brutality of the police than Chaplin must ever have intended to insert. *Modern Times,* after all, was really of a piece with the other Chaplin work, and should have been criticized within the framework of the Chaplin history, rather than a new time. His cops were the same old cops, kicking the poor around—nothing new about that in the Chaplin work. Nobody ever complained that Mack Sennett was showing the police and the forces of justice in an unjust way.

Modern Times was ubiquitous: the right-wing saw a red hand at work, the moderates saw a confused philosophy, the left-wing saw a 'bitterly satirical cartoon' against modern capitalism; the Russians saw none of these things, not even enough to praise the film, but the Nazis and Fascists, who were using the same 'factory' techniques, banned the film. Many critics were puzzled by the film, because they expected more than it delivered. But the lasting effect was the most telling: anyone who saw the assembly line scenes in *Modern Times* was not likely to forget them.

When the critics began, Chaplin at first denied any 'social significance' in his work. He was a clown, he said, and it was his intent to entertain the world with his pictures. But as the attacks continued beyond the normal critical phase, Chaplin's own views of his work were either created or solidified. He had approached the film with an idea, he said, a desire to show how industrial society prescribed the rights of the individual. This was certainly anything but communism—nihilism or anarchism, but not communism. But a nervous managerial society in America had bracketed Chaplin as an enemy of 'the system' and the criticism was never to cease from this point on. As it became more fierce, ending in boycotts and threatening Chaplin's position and livelihood, he responded with stronger statements of his own, and the pyramid of hatred and distrust began to build.

Modern Times was, as always, a financial success, although Chaplin expected more than the nearly two million dollars the film grossed in America, he probably should not have expected so much. In the year 1936 the original impetus of America recovery had slackened off, and the economy of the

United States was sliding again. Europe was not only more receptive to the ideas of the film, but seemed to be in better economic condition to receive it, so Chaplin prospered financially once again.

When *Modern Times* was out of the way Chaplin wanted a change and some peace from the Press. The only way he could get it at times when a new picture put him in the limelight, he found, was to travel by ship. He and Paulette Goddard headed for the Orient. On the trip they were married, although for reasons of their own they kept this fact secret. Paulette had been living in the Beverly Hills mansion for a long time anyhow, and perhaps they did not wish to draw attention to themselves; Chaplin did not need the publicity.

What he did need was an idea for a new film that he could make successfully, given the overwhelming turn to talking pictures. He was convinced by this time that he could no longer continue to impress the market with silent films, even when he added sound effects and music. But what could he do that would not destroy the little fellow?

Actually, the Chaplin 'era' was over. A new generation did not even remember the old two-reelers and one-reelers that had made Chaplin famous. The comedy they were used to had become much more sophisticated. The ways of the past could be attuned to the era; W. C. Fields was showing that by adapting his old juggler's tricks to the talking pictures. But Fields also talked, and his talk was an integral part of his comedy action. Chaplin was making few concessions to the modern taste, probably because he still believed that Charlie, the little fellow, could not survive the transition.

Another factor had entered the entertainment field; the film world was subject to politicization. World depression, the rise of dictatorships, and the diverging of the world into opposing theories and systems of government brought political propaganda to the motion pictures.

Chaplin was accused by some critics of taking a revolutionary point of view in the factory and mob scenes of *Modern Times*. On the other side, the Russian communists did not much care for the film. But those of political bent read into it what they wanted, in spite of Chaplin's flat disclaimer that he had any end in mind except entertainment. The world had changed, there was no question about it, and any social commentary at all, even spoofing, would arouse its own group of enemies. *Modern Times* was banned in Nazi Germany and Fascist Italy. They said it was communist. It was actually 'individualistic', the same little character continued his same old battle against the forces of authority and repression that he had been losing for years. *Modern Times* did not do well in America, although it showed a profit, but abroad it was more successful, partly perhaps because of the bannings.

What Chaplin came up with was a Hitler picture. Hitler had the tramp's moustache, and with the proper haircut and a drab uniform, Chaplin could pass for Hitler at a hundred feet almost anywhere. Using the tried technique of the double, he could play Hitler and a little fellow. What littler fellow was there in Germany than a Jew? So the little fellow became a Jewish barber, for this film. It was, of course, a departure. The little fellow had always played himself before, but it could be done, and Chaplin decided it would be done. Chaplin began work on a screenplay.

In the summer of 1939 the script was finished and the techniques established, the set was ready and the casting was in progress. Paulette Goddard would play the feminine lead. Jack Oakie would play Napaloni, the other dictator. Chaplin would play the oppressor and the oppressed.

Then, when all was begun, the Nazis marched into Poland. Everything stopped at the Chaplin studio, while he reconsidered the marketing problem. Was an audience going to think that Hitler was funny, with men dying and the tide of tyranny rising? Chaplin considered this problem very seriously. In the end he decided to go ahead.

The techniques of filming *The Great Dictator* were completely different from those Chaplin had used in his previous films. It was to be a talking picture, even though the dialogue was to be kept to a minimum so that foreign audiences would gain the full import. Thus the approach must be different. What had been said by gesture before, was now said by word many times, and that was a much slower and less comprehensive way of making a statement.

The Great Dictator opened with a scene that might have
been taken from *Shoulder Arms*—a battlefield. Big Bertha, the
giant German field gun, was ready to fire on the Cathedral
of Notre Dame. The gunner, Charlie in an oversize helmet
and ill-fitting uniform, pulled the lanyard and grabbed his
binoculars, to see the shell fall—on an outhouse.

In the next scene, Charlie, the German soldier, manned an
anti-aircraft gun, then got mixed up in trench warfare and
got a grenade down his trouser leg. Next he was piloting a
plane, and crashing it. And then the war was over. Tomania,
his country, had lost.

A newspaper montage brought the picture into the 1930s,
as the Dictator Adenoid Hynkel took power. The little
barber was in hospital, suffering from amnesia.

In the next scene, Dictator Hynkel was making a speech to
a huge crowd of the followers of the Double Cross. Chaplin
used Germanic doubletalk to ape Hitler's speech style perfectly.

Before he started filming, Chaplin began to feel considerable heat inside and outside the industry. The word
came from Britain that a comedy about Hitler would be
badly received. As the shooting continued, Chaplin began to
receive hate mail, and to become worried about what might
happen before the picture was finished or afterward. Yet he
persisted. He would finish the film and he would show it.
Later he would say that if he had known the full extent of
Hitler's crimes against humanity—the extermination of the
Jews and subject peoples—he would never have been able to
finish the film. But the world was unaware of the full enormity of Hitler, and Chaplin knew no more than anyone else.

Goering was Herring, the fat general with all the comic
possibilities that implied. Goebbels was Garbitsch with all
that implied.

Almost immediately Hynkel launched a campaign against
the Jews, as Hannah, the girl, was introduced, and then the
little barber returned from hospital to open his shop, believing that just a few weeks had passed since he went to war.
Hannah and the barber were beset by storm-troopers, and
fought them off. But the barber was captured and being
hanged on a lamp-post when an old war friend whose life he

had saved came up. The friend was now a Nazi leader. The barber was saved.

At Hynkel's palace the dictator was busy, with a flunkey even licking his envelopes for him. Herring brought in the inventor of a new bullet-proof suit, Hynkel tested it by shooting at the inventor, who fell down dead. Hynkel was annoyed with the waste of his time. A little more byplay, and Herring returned with the inventor of a new parachute. The inventor jumped out the window, Hynkel and Herring leaned out, then Hynkel again complained that Herring wasted his time.

Garbitsch and Hynkel discussed the Jewish problem. They changed policy while they negotiated a loan with a Jewish banker. It was obvious the policy would change back almost immediately.

The scene shifted to the little barber and the girl, hoping for happiness and giving the little fellow a chance for some pure comedy of the old Chaplin variety. But it was back to Hynkel again soon enough, with Herring bouncing in with a new invention, a poison gas guaranteed to kill everybody.

Hynkel, surrounded by sycophants, insisted on being alone, and then to music began to play with a globe that was really a huge balloon, making a ballet of it. It was one of the most telling scenes of Chaplin's career, combining his grace and agility as a dancer, and his superb mastery of the art of pantomime.

The film cut back and forth from dictator to barber, the plot progressing as Hynkel became ever more oppressive, and finally got rid of Schultz, the barber's one Aryan friend. But Schultz escaped and sought refuge with the Jews. Schultz and the barber were captured and sent to prison. Meanwhile Hynkel wanted to invade Austerlich but was afraid of what his fellow dictator Napaloni might do. The meetings between Hynkel and Napaloni were a classic of comedy, depending far more on the old Chaplin silent techniques than on the talk.

In a complicated mix-up, Hynkel and the little barber exchanged identities, Hynkel was dragged off to the concentration camp while the barber was taken to invade Austerlich. And at the end of the film, Chaplin stepped completely out of character and, as the barber impersonating Hynkel, he gave a six-minute peroration against dictatorship and man's inhumanity to man.

The Great Dictator was finished and released in the fall of 1940, when the United States was in the throes of a new determination of policy. All the old adages dealing with non-intervention and non-alignment with any blocs were still in the air. The Nazis were spending millions to try to keep America out of the war, even though the Roosevelt administration was doing all it could, short of war, to assist the allies. Chaplin's film, then, dropped into the controversy like a bomb, and was hailed or hated depending on the political views of the cinema-goer.

By 1940, as the sharp light of publicity became personal, Chaplin also had become extremely sensitive to criticism—he was getting so much of it, for his personal life, his pictures, and his political opinions. He quarrelled often with the Press and with many leaders of American opinion, who were inclined to regard Hitler as a relatively minor evil. In his sensitivity he refused awards for *The Great Dictator,* and these refusals labelled him a 'sorehead' and added to the conflict. A long time had passed since Chaplin was the idol of all America. The idyll had ended and there was no question about it.

13

Purgatory

Charles Chaplin and Paulette Goddard parted in 1940 and were never really together again, although it was nearly two years before Miss Goddard obtained a Mexican divorce from Chaplin. In the interim, Chaplin's public image suffered from his bouts with the Press, and from the mixed reaction to *The Great Dictator*. The film created some sparks in inter-American relations, particularly between the United States and Latin-American countries that were maintaining either a real neutrality or were leaning toward the Nazis.

Chaplin was torn. Sometimes he said he had wanted to make nothing more than a comedy about dictators. Sometimes he said he had a social purpose in mind. "I made *The Great Dictator* because I hate dictators and I want people to laugh," he said one day.

The problems were not entirely political. Chaplin had made a very large fortune from films through their distribution in America and abroad. His financial affairs were extremely complicated, and the American tax authorities said that he owed the federal government much more than he felt he owed. Such considerations led to conflict and to a feeling on the part of the taxpayer that the government was picking on him. Then the war brought Chaplin's relations with America to a crisis.

One day in the summer of 1942 Charles Chaplin was asked to make a speech in San Francisco on behalf of Russian war relief. He accepted, and in his ringing speech he called for the opening of a second front against the Nazis by the Western allies.

Charles Chaplin knew nothing at all about military strategy and tactics, and had never pretended to know anything.

His appeal was purely emotional: the Russians were fighting the Nazis; the Russians wanted a second front; the Western powers should attack. How this was to be done with the materials at hand was a question that Chaplin simply did not consider. He was concerned because so many around him were saying of the Russians and Nazis: a pox on both their houses. He continued his speeches and statements in this vein that summer and autumn. In so doing, Chaplin touched a sore nerve in the West. The alliance between America and Britain on the one hand and Soviet Russia on the other was a fragile affair, based on mutual need and a mutual fear of damnation and defeat if they did not unite. The Russians did not trust the Westerners, and the West did not trust the Russians. Chaplin's espousal of the Russian cause was heartfelt and sincere, but taken with his views on political economy, it was largely misinterpreted and made fodder for his enemies. The number of those enemies had grown, and would grow, embracing almost the entire right fringe of American life, and including more and more organizations, as time went on.

The divorce of 1942 brought Chaplin considerable pain. Miss Goddard received £350,000 worth of jewellery in the settlement, and then went her own way, to succeed in films and to marry Burgess Meredith, the actor. Chaplin soon became involved with another young woman, Joan Barry, in the most unfortunate liaison he had ever made. He was thinking about a new film, and about a new leading lady. The film did not materialize into a motion-picture project for Chaplin, although he did pursue it for some time. But in the middle of his preliminary work, Orson Welles suggested to him a film based on the French lady-killer Landru, and Chaplin was so intrigued he bought the idea from Welles and began to work on it. Meanwhile he had quarrelled with Joan Barry and she had gone out of his life. It had been the stormiest of Chaplin's love affairs. At one point Miss Barry had threatened to commit suicide. He had her arrested after one scene and given a suspended sentence to leave Los Angeles. She came back and he had her arrested again after she made her way into his house, and she served thirty days, mostly in a sanitarium.

Meanwhile Chaplin had met Oona O'Neill, the eighteen-year-old daughter of playwright Eugene O'Neill, and apparently an aspiring actress. She and Chaplin got on famously, and were soon seen together all over Hollywood. Miss O'Neill might be Chaplin's new leading lady, was the gossip in Hollywood. But instead, in the spring of 1943, she became Mrs Charles Chaplin, and immediately retired from the motion-picture industry.

In the 1940s Charles Chaplin seemed to be forever in the public eye in ways that did nothing for his art or his position in American society. After *Modern Times* he was sued twice for plagiarism by people who said he had lifted ideas or sequences of the film from them. Both suits were eventually dismissed but not before they had done their harm. After *The Great Dictator* Chaplin was sued by screen writer Konrad Bercovici for taking the theme of the motion picture from a presentation offered by the writer. That suit was settled out of court. Miss Barry sued Chaplin for support as the father of a child born to her, and this dragged through the courts. Meanwhile he was assaulted by his enemies in another way; government lawyers went before a federal grand-jury and had him indicted for violation of the Mann Act and denial of Miss Barry's civil rights. The Mann Act was a morality law of a nature peculiar to America. It was enacted to halt the transfer of prostitutes from one of the American states to another; it was used in later years by federal authorities as a sort of catch-all to try to pin charges on persons considered enemies of the state.

Chaplin was in 1943 a worried man, and he showed it by seeking the services of Jerry Giesler, one of America's foremost trial lawyers, to defend him. Again he could not have taken an action more likely to arouse the attention of the Press. A Giesler trial always had the possibility of drama. Add to that the fame of the defendant, and the sensational nature of the charges, and the elements were present for high scandal.

The paternity case was given special drama when Chaplin and the child took blood tests, and it was determined that he could not be the father according to the tests. Yet the court found against Chaplin, and ordered him to pay child support.

The criminal case aroused even more attention if possible, but when the jury considered the government's charges, Chaplin was found innocent on all counts. Artistic life was really no better for Chaplin after that. Whatever was left of innocence in the Western world after one great war and a terrible depression vanished in the second war. Chaplin's camera was stilled during the war years. He was under fire by the tax authorities, because he was considered to be the richest man in Hollywood. As simply as his little Charlie, he took the war and the Grand Alliance of the Western world with the Soviet Union quite seriously, and threw himself into propagandizing for a second front (which the Russians wanted) and for total assistance to the Russians in their fight against Germany.

He was in way over his head, and the more politically he became involved, the more enemies he earned. By war's end, the image of Charles Chaplin in America was badly tarnished. There would be no more Chaplin dolls or Chaplin songs and very little Chaplin praise. Ironically, in spite of the virtual destruction of his film career, Chaplin was embarked on the happiest period of his life. Oona O'Neill was another embodiment of Chaplin's endless vision of youth, she was dark and beautiful and eighteen years old, but she had absolutely no interest in acting or even the social world. She wanted nothing more than to be wife to Chaplin and mother to his children.

From 1945 on, Chaplin was under heavy fire in America. As Western relations with Russia worsened, his own words were used against him, and stubbornly he refused to do the only thing that might have saved him, recant and retire to solitude. Instead he spoke out. Enemies accused him of being a communist. He denied it flatly. He was baited for not taking out American citizenship. He said he was citizen of the world. When old friends came under attack he tried to help them, although some of them were communists or former communists. The Press attacked Chaplin even more furiously, on many grounds: moral turpitude, left-wing leanings, failure to become an American citizen. The war against Chaplin was declared. Much of the Press set out to destroy him. The radical right-wing of Congress also leaped into the struggle, and Rep. John Rankin of Mississippi called his movies "loathsome pictures".

It is astounding and depressing to contemplate the change in America that brought about the fall of this folk-hero. Yet the seeds were always there; Chaplin had simply made them grow. The hysteria that gripped America claimed many victims; he was only one of them, although the most prominent. He was damned for his non-conformity.

Into this poisonous atmosphere of America in near terror, in 1946 Chaplin launched an entirely different type of film from any of his previous pictures. It was *Monsieur Verdoux,* suggested by the career of Landru, the celebrated French murderer of women. Charlie was gone, and in his place came a suave man of the world, with a waxed moustache. For the first time Chaplin admittedly set out to lampoon the times; he suggested in an interview that murder was the logical extension of business, and thus his theme. He was in some views, biting the hand that fed him.

In his early features, up to *The Great Dictator,* Charles Chaplin had so centred his films around his own character that he needed few professional actors and even those were given largely one-dimensional roles. He had kept much of his acting crew together over the years. But the more complex pictures demanded another treatment; he had employed well-known performers in *The Great Dictator,* and he did so again in *Monsieur Verdoux.* His choice of theme, the universal matter of murder, indicates the complexity to which Chaplin had risen in his mature years. He must have known even as he planned and made the film, what a far cry it was from the little fellow of *Shoulder Arms* and *The Kid.* And, for the first time, Chaplin made straight and unabashed use of sound in this film.

Monsieur Verdoux opened with Chaplin speaking, in fact. His voice was superimposed on a close-up of *Verdoux's* tombstone, as he explained how he had been a bank clerk who married women for their money and then killed them. It was strictly a business for him, he said, conducted to support his household. There was no passion involved.

The film then began to delve into *Monsieur Verdoux's* life and techniques, beginning with a scene of the Couvais family, one of whose female members had gone off with Verdoux after drawing all her money out of the bank. They were suspicious—but no more than that.

Verdoux was then seen in a rose garden in Southern France, with an incinerator smoking behind him—the sublime and the monstrous, for the incinerator contained the mortal remains of Thelma Couvais. He moved inside the house, accepted a letter for Thelma, forged her signature, and counted out the last of the money from her account. Then he sat down, this gentleman of leisure, to play a rhapsody on the piano. A new cook arrived, then he telephoned his broker to buy some stocks.

In Paris, the plot had thickened. Lena Couvais had told the police that her sister married and immediately disappeared, taking all her money. So had twelve other women, the police informed her, all women past the prime of beauty, all women with large property. Obviously, a murderer was loose.

Back at the villa the widow Marie Grosnay called on Verdoux with an estate agent. When he learned that she was a widow he began pursuing her about the room, while the agent was elsewhere. On the agent's return the ageing suitor concealed his ardour by chasing a bee. Then came a bit of the old Chaplin foolishness—Verdoux slipped and fell out the window in his pursuit of the 'bee'. But he recovered sufficiently to present this new prospect with a bouquet of roses before she left the place.

In the next sequence, Verdoux was in Paris, where he encountered old acquaintances and showed off a roll of bills. "You must have made a killing!" said the old friend. Indeed, said Verdoux, the one-time bank clerk who had come so far. He passed on to his office, and there had the sobering news that his margin accounts were in danger. He must produce 50,000 francs swiftly or he would be ruined.

Out came the little book, and soon Verdoux was on the way to the house of Lydia Floray. He greeted her romantically, but this middle-aged woman wanted none of that. He then got down to her interests: he had a tip that the banks were threatened and next day there would be a run on them. He just happened to know that Lydia's bank closed at four o'clock. She erupted in excitement, and told him to get her 70,000 francs before it was too late.

And he did. That night Verdoux rhapsodized at the piano and then on the balcony, as Lydia growled at him to go to bed. He did that too. Next morning, he carelessly set two places for breakfast, then thoughtfully removed one of them.

The film then jumped to a cottage in the countryside, and to Verdoux's real home with his wife and son. It was their tenth anniversary, he was looking forward to the day he could retire from business.

So far this fare had been heavy with drama and establishment of character. Next Verdoux went to visit his 'wife' Annabella Bonheur. Here he was matched with that great *comédienne* Martha Raye, obviously an intended victim. He bought a vial of chloroform for her, but they quarrelled and he had no chance to use it. Immediately the busy businessman was off on another chase, after Mme Grosnay, who had spurned him in spite of his roses. But only briefly, back to the chemist's to discuss poisons, and then a fine new formula that left no trace. Wanting to try it out he picked up a prostitute, but she beguiled him with a tale of an unhappy marriage, and he let her go.

Arrested by a policeman on fourteen counts of murder, Verdoux gave the poison intended for the girl to the officer. He killed two birds with one stone, tested his formula and escaped the law.

Back with Miss Raye, Verdoux did all he could to destroy her. Poison—the maid used as hair bleach. Chloroform—he chloroformed himself. A rock and a rope—he nearly drowned.

Chasing Mme Grosnay again, his technique began to work, but as it worked, the stock market crashed, and he was wiped out. Soon, the audience learned that he lost also his wife and child.

In Paris Verdoux discovered the girl he had befriended; she was now riding in a limousine, she had married a rich munitions manufacturer. That was the business he should have been in, said Verdoux. That was where the money was.

And then, as Verdoux spoke, his destiny arrived. Lena Couvais and the detectives arrived to collar him, he escaped for a short hilarious session of old Chaplin chase, but in the end he was captured. And then came trial, at which Verdoux suggested that the world was guilty of mass murder, why was he singled out? In prison he pursued the philosophic line with a reporter who came to interview the mass murderer. But no, said Verdoux, the single murderer was a villain, the murderer of millions became a hero. A priest came and Verdoux teased him, and then the gaolers. They offered him rum, at first he refused, then he accepted because he had never tasted rum. And with that last little relish of life, the hands were tied, the door opened, and Verdoux marched to the guillotine.

Monsieur Verdoux was released in the spring of 1947. By that time Chaplin's life in America was sheer torment. The Cold War between the Western powers and the Soviet bloc had begun to freeze the year before, and all Chaplin's past defences of Soviet Russia and the Soviet society were remembered. Chaplin would not budge from his previous positions; he was forced to deny that he was a communist, and then his enemies called him a crypto-communist. Theoretically, the quarrel of American society with communism related to the conspiratorial nature of the communist party and its dedication to forcible overthrow of the government. By extension, in 1947, many American citizens who had praised Soviet Russia were brought under deep suspicion. Chaplin, not a citizen, had stoutly refused to seek American citizenship, and this decision brought him the enmity of super-patriots. Church groups and other organizations dedicated to the maintenance of public morality detested Chaplin after the Barry paternity case and the Mann Act trial. In court he was called a master seducer and a cheap Cockey cad. Outside the epithets did not become more gentle. And with the appearance of *Monsieur Verdoux* the American wing of the Roman Catholic Church took offence at the treatment of the priest and of marriage. One could not make fun of murder. The Church organized a boycott that was effective and disastrous to the film, helped along by many critics who reviewed Chaplin rather than the art, and by many of the old enemies. After a quarter of a century of determined individualism on the screen and off, Chaplin had earned an impressive list of foes.

Those who hated Chaplin detested the film, and found in it most of the objections they had to the man. Hedda Hopper, the film columnist, predicted that this was the end of Chaplin. The film was barred by censors and picketed by pressure groups. Worst of all, it was ignored by most of the film-going public.

With the intellectual group in America, the film was also controversial. James Agee, Chaplin's friend and *Time* movie reviewer, declared it to be Chaplin's finest work, but the respected Howard Barnes of the New York *Herald Tribune* called it an insult to the intelligence. Some found it preachy, obvious, and naïve. The munitions makers had been thoroughly roasted many times before by Upton Sinclair and others, and so had the apposition of government crimes with individual criminality been stated.

The American reaction ranged from banning to lavish praise, but there was not enough of the latter to counteract the forces that worked against the film. For the first time, Loew's theatres reported, a Chaplin film actually lost money. It was the same in most areas of the country. The major force working against the picture was Charles Chaplin's position in American society in 1947. That much became clear when Chaplin met the Press to promote the picture. He was attacked by a representative of the Catholic War Veterans in the conference, not because of the film but because he had not become an American citizen. He was attacked by other newspaper reporters as a fellow traveller. He was asked if he was a communist. A great segment of the American press, including the newspapers of his old friend William Randolph Hearst, suggested that Chaplin ought to be expelled from the United States not for his art, but for his political views.

He was called to appear before the Un-American Activities Committee of the House of Representatives along with some twenty other Hollywood personalities, including the German composer Hanns Eisler who was a good friend of Chaplins. But on this occasion Chaplin sent the House committee a telegram, stating that he was not a communist, did not belong to any party or organization, and was what he called a "peacemonger".

The attacks in America redoubled. The American Legion denounced him as a traitor to America. Westbrook Pegler, the newspaper-columnist, began one of his vendettas against Chaplin. These were notable for their continuity and ascerbity. Chaplin was called "a damned communist Jew" in places where that sort of language was used, and it did him no good to deny that he was either communist or a Jew. Even old admirers like Parker Tyler wondered if *Monsieur Verdoux* was not somehow Chaplin's request to public opinion to forgive him his "sex-trespasses as it forgives the war trespasses of the capitalists".

Abroad, the reaction was quite different except in Soviet Russia, where he was denounced as "a traitor to the working class". But in France, the French Association of Cinema Critics proposed unanimously that Chaplin be given the Nobel Peace Prize for his last three films, including *Monsieur Verdoux*. The film was a success in Europe, and won critical praise and public applause which could be translated into recovery at the box office, but the film never did nearly so well as Chaplin had hoped.

The nadir of Chaplin's career began in 1947. When a Congressional committee moved to deport Hanns Eisler, Chaplin was in touch with another communist friend, Pablo Picasso, asking him to head a protest committee. Senator Harry P. Cain found this action so reprehensible on Chaplin's part that he demanded Chaplin himself be deported.

And thus was an idea born.

14

Limelight

Before the end of the 1940s the complete Chaplin had emerged and was being tested in the merciless heat of an aroused American public opinion. Chaplin's own stubborn statements and the Press reporting of them tended to complicate the relatively simple philosophy of a dedicated artist. That is not to say that Chaplin was ever a simple character; on the contrary he was extremely complex. He was given to moods: sometimes he was introspective and avoided people, at other times he sought the crowd. Sometimes he was generous, sometimes he was stingy. His lonely youth carried over, and in Hollywood he often had fits of solitude. He was nearly paralyzed by crowds in the early years, yet he learned to live with them, but he never did learn completely to deal with the Press. He was a very private person, and the Press was no respecter of privacy. Further, his relationships with people often ran from one extreme to another; in a way he was something like the millionaire in *Modern Times* who could only remember the little fellow when he was drunk. Chaplin would welcome a new acquaintance as a bosom friend, and then suddenly dart away from him or her. When he was making *City Lights,* suddenly for no apparent reason he fired two of his old associates out of hand. Later he fired Carl Robinson, his press agent for sixteen years. He was subject to moments of joyous abandon, and then to fits of temper in which he lashed viciously at the object of his annoyance. By his own statement, he was extremely emotional, and impetuous; characteristics proved out by his many affairs of the heart and four marriages.

The artistic Chaplin stemmed from this emotionalism; so

did the 'political' Chaplin. His base was the lowest common denominator of humanity, the little fellow. Championing the underdog came completely naturally to him, from his own underdog childhood. It may be indicative that in America, where every segment of society has exploited black humour, Chaplin would never do so. The blacks had suffered so much throughout history that Chaplin found it impossible to make jokes that involved blacks.

By nature Chaplin was the anarchist, the rebel against strictures. This facet of character first showed itself in his personal life; he would not live or even pretend to live, by the rules of a puritan society. Time after time this particular bit of independence cost him dearly, yet he continued to go his own way. In politics, from the outset he championed the Bolsheviks. So did many others. He did continue to champion the Soviets through World War II and after, when many who had accepted Soviet rule by force were falling off that wagon. As the evils of Soviet society were uncovered and exposed to the West, Chaplin continued to stand fast for Russia because he believed in certain basic philosophies. Repeatedly he said he was not a communist, nor did he belong to any political party. He did believe in the philosophical principles of communism, in the broadest scale: the sharing of the world's goods, the brotherhood of man. Never having to live under state socialism, he did not have to contend with its restrictive qualities, and he refused to be caught up in argument about them. This evasion of what the anti-communists considered to be a basic issue turned many of them against Chaplin in the 1940s and 1950s, and a good deal more was sometimes read into his last few films than he could have intended. For the secret of Chaplin's comedy, and Chaplin's pathos, was his exposure of human frailties in the broadest terms. Chinese Taoists, Egyptian Muslims and Indian Zoroastrians could laugh as heartily at the Chaplin motion pictures as could any citizen of London or New York. This universality really ended with *Modern Times,* although Chaplin kept alive part of his technique in *The Great Dictator.* But with *Monsieur Verdoux* the multi-cultural was sacrificed, and the rest of Chaplin's films would be aimed primarily at a highly sophisticated audience.

The period of Chaplin's most unhappy public life coincided with the beginning of personal happiness. His marriage to Oona O'Neill could not have been more idyllic. The Press approached the marriage as another of Chaplin's forays into the yard of youth—and the Press could not have been more wrong. The fifty-four-year-old bridegroom and the eighteen-year-old bride were ideally matched. Oona had a quality of dealing with people that completely disarmed the Press. On her wedding day she was asked the brutal question: why had she chosen a man three times her own age, moreover a notorious figure with a scandalous reputation? It was, she said "an esoteric union". While the reporter involved rushed back to the office to look up esoteric, the new Mrs Chaplin retreated into a glass cocoon from which she never emerged as far as the Press was concerned. Years later Michael Chaplin would recall a part of the secret: "Mother was a mistress of the gentle art of making them feel relaxed; at least it seemed that way to me whenever I saw her listening to my father's slightest anecdotage, even when I knew perfectly well that she'd heard it a hundred times before...." There seemed no way to get at her; she was a wife and she became a mother, she loved her husband and she was interested in raising a family. That sort of 'news' does not satisfy very many editors.

Oona moved into the big house in Beverly Hills and settled down to raise a family. She created precisely what Chaplin wanted, a real home, and she ministered to his wants as no other woman had done. A visitor in the afternoon to the Chaplin house was not nearly so likely to get a gin and tonic or a martini as a high tea. The Chaplins lived quietly, without ostentation, entertained friends, and stayed out of the public glare, as much as Chaplin could ever do in America.

Soon the children began to come along. Geraldine was the first, then came Michael, Josephine, and Victoria. They grew up in the world of celebrities. William Tilden came by to play tennis with Chaplin, and young Michael's best friend was the son of Charles Boyer. But they were as unspoiled as Hollywood children could ever be; Chaplin was a stern disciplinarian and sometimes his temper got the best of him.

He had no qualms about spanking. The children went to private day-schools but they were no more isolated than the children of other families of similar means.

In 1950 Chaplin was working on *Limelight,* the new motion picture that had occurred to him. He said he still had confidence that the American people would rise above the pettiness of the hysterical years of the late 1940s and early 1950s. As much trouble as he had encountered with *Monsieur Verdoux* he still believed he had a large audience in the United States; and he knew he had a large audience elsewhere.

For *Limelight,* Chaplin reached deep into his own past. Rumour had it that he was basing the film on the life of Mark Sheridan, a very popular English music-hall entertainer who had enjoyed a spectacular career, but in the end had shot himself. These were the days of T. E. Dunville, Arthur Reece, and Charles Godfrey. The tragedy of Sheridan's life had been his loss of the spark that drew the English people to him, and he had killed himself in the belief that he had failed, and had lost his public.

Perhaps the Sheridan story did trigger some instinct in Chaplin. The story he chose to tell was not dissimilar; the hero, Calvero, was an ageing music hall comedian who wanted to make a comeback after years of obscurity, but he had lost his confidence, and was haunted by the fact that he had also lost the capacity of making people laugh. He fell in love with a young ballerina who shared his fear; he saved her from killing herself, he helped her conquer the fear, and yet his own fear continued. And in the end, Calvero lost the girl to the young composer she really loved.

So here were the old Chaplin elements in a modern setting. The comedian—no longer the little fellow but Chaplin himself in his mature middle age—the beautiful girl, the cruel world, and the ultimate sacrifice.

The film opened on a scene of a London street, with a barrel organ and children—something straight out of Chaplin's childhood. The girl had decided to commit suicide, and the camera next focused on her in the miserable lodging-house room, poison vial in hand, gas stove turned on. Then it cut to Calvero, coming drunkenly up the street.

Calvero saved the girl. Then he talked to her about the beauty of life. In this sense *Limelight* was the logical progression for Chaplin in the medium. For years he had exploited the possibilities of the silent film, only gradually coming to grips with the 'words business'. *Limelight* is a talky film in that sense; Chaplin was having his say about life.

Other characters intruded, the hefty landlady, the street urchins outside, the performers of Calvero's world, the composer, but as always the film was Chaplin's shared with Claire Bloom—but always with Chaplin dominant. He was so dominant that the reviews scarcely mentioned Miss Bloom or the others, they concentrated on the many facets of Chaplin in this most complex of all his films.

It is hard to realize how resilient is genius even in the declining years. For *Limelight* Chaplin embarked on an entirely new skill—choreography, and he did it well enough to rate critical acclaim from the professionals. During the making of the film he visited New York and Constance Collier gave a tea party for him. In came Markova and Dolin, on their way back with their ballet to London, and Chaplin began talking about the ballet sequence of *Limelight*—and pantomiming *The Death of Columbine,* the ballet he was creating. His dance was so vivid that the two famous dancers promised right there they would dance it for him. They did not, other engagements prevented it, but in that meeting they had asked only one question—when?

He had become a choreographer then, although in the credits on the screen he gave Andre Eglevsky and Milissa Dayden equal billing in this department. And choreography was only a part of what he personally accomplished, in this most ambitious of all his projects. Chaplin was producer of the film. Chaplin was director of the film. Chaplin wrote the story and then the screenplay. Chaplin wrote the music. Chaplin wrote the songs. Chaplin played the lead.

There were in addition, many Chaplins in the film, spanning two generations. In spite of the unpleasantness of his divorce from Lita Grey, Chaplin managed to restore some sanity to their relationship in time. Lita and Paulette Goddard met a few times, and were cordial to one another. Chaplin saw something of his two boys, Charles Jr, and

Sydney in their formative years, and as they came to manhood they became quite friendly. They were protected in their youth from the glare of publicity that dogged Chaplin, but both went into the theatrical business in time. Both served in the American army in World War II, also, a fact that Chaplin might have trumpeted to the world during his years of crisis, when his 'patriotism' was questioned. He mentioned it once or twice, but never attempted to use the boys for his purposes.

In *Limelight* both elder Chaplin children had parts. Sydney's was the largest, he played the role of Nevile. Charles Jr, had a smaller part as a clown. Then, also, the three eldest of the new Chaplin children had roles in the motion picture; Geraldine, Michael, and Josephine played children.

In every way, the making of *Limelight* was a happy period for the Chaplins. Once he had been accused of abandoning Edna Purviance, his old leading lady of years past. The public did not know that Chaplin kept her on the payroll and would for the rest of her life.

Abandoned? Here she was in *Limelight,* in a bit role, but in the picture. Even when criticized Chaplin never offered the obvious defence that Edna Purviance had grown too old to continue as his leading lady, nor did he tell the world the efforts he had made fruitlessly to spur her career as an actress after *A Woman of Paris.*

Limelight was the most emotional of the Chaplin films, the most philosophical, the most 'artistic' in the modern film sense. Chaplin was always a student of the cinematographic art, in this film he employed Karl Struss as chief of photography, with Rollie Totheroh, his old cameraman from the silent days, as film consultant. He had an associate director and associate producers, and an editor.

The poignancy of *Limelight* hit a new level, for in other films usually at the end did the little fellow come face to face with tragedy. In *Limelight,* after Calvero had saved the girl and persuaded her that life was beautiful, she believed she was in love with him. Knowing the truth, Calvero ran away to become a beggar, while she rose to fame. And then tragedy was reasserted. In the end, Calvero's friends gave a benefit for him, and Terry danced, as Calvero died, the lonely pathetic clown, having achieved the measure of dignity to which he aspired.

Early in 1952, foreign writers visiting Chaplin in Hollywood had the impression that the years of strife had come to an end. They saw a happy Chaplin, moving between the studio and the house, wrapped up in his work and his family. It was five years since the release of *Monsieur Verdoux,* and the Press seemed to have relaxed.

When the film was finished, Chaplin decided to take an exploratory trip to Europe. For some time he had been thinking about leaving Hollywood. For one thing, he had been deeply burned by the events and charges of the late 1940s, and at various times had written or said that he might very well leave. There was another factor in 1952—many Hollywood personalities were leaving to seek tax refuge in the 'cheap' countries of Europe. Many of the major film studios were shut down or leased out to television production, which seemed to threaten movie-making with oblivion. Chaplin was not sure. He was thinking seriously of putting his children in school in Europe, to remove them from the hysterical anti-communist atmosphere of the United States. He had the definite feeling that the American environment was unhealthy.

Oona and the children were American citizens, and there was no problem of travel for them. Chaplin, still holding his British passport, must secure a re-entry permit although he had lived in America for many years. To make sure his tax affairs were in good order, he filed and paid. The Internal Revenue Service tried to charge him for extra tax, he took the case to court, and secured a settlement of that claim, and there seemed nothing to stop him from going abroad and returning to Beverly Hills at his convenience. There was delay in securing the re-entry permit, and finally Chaplin indicated that he was going to leave with it or without it, and then it was granted after a three-hour questioning.

All seemed well, but Chaplin's sense of self-preservation led him to convert many of his assets into readily negotiable securities, and he put these in a safe deposit box in Los Angeles. Further, he made certain that Oona would have access to the box. Then he made ready to take the trip on which he would decide about the future.

In New York, the Chaplins visited friends and he made a few attempts to promote *Limelight,* but it was nothing like the old days when Charles Chaplin could not move from his hotel without being mobbed by Press and public. He went virtually unnoticed. The last few days were irritating; he was being sued and his lawyers tried to keep him in his hotel to avoid process servers. He did go to a Press preview of *Limelight* and he felt the unfriendliness of the atmosphere, then on the day of sailing, he had to sneak aboard the *Queen Elizabeth* early in the morning and hide to avoid process servers. (He was being sued again by a dissatisfied employee.) It was neither a dignified nor a happy way to leave the country, he really had no opportunity to test the reactions to *Limelight* in America. Since the film was totally non-political, and could not even be accused of immorality, there should be no reason for any segment of American society to rouse a hate campaign against the film. As his friends were saying, the days of controversy should be ended in these golden years.

But the time was September, 1952. In the United States an election campaign was in process, one of those long gruelling struggles that decides whether the Republican or Democratic wing of the American Institution shall execute the laws of the land with its particular bias for the next four years. The candidates were the great compromiser Dwight D. Eisenhower, and the liberal intellectual Adlai Stevenson. The issue chosen as basic by the Republicans was the senility of Democratic rule for twenty years, and the major proof items were moral corruption and 'softness on communism'—which meant failure to be sufficiently anti-communist.

The opening of a new Charles Chaplin film in this atmosphere turned out to be disastrous. No matter the film, was not Chaplin the despoiler of young American womanhood, and the secret agent of revolution against the establishment? Chaplin was too valuable a political asset for the Republicans to leave him alone. As any politician knew, he was an excellent target because it was hard for him to fight back, and harrying Chaplin was at various times of his career something of a national journalistic sport. (In 1946 he had testified that he believed ninety-five per cent of the American newspapers were against him.)

In the past few years Chaplin had managed to remain quiet. There was little publicity about him in 1948. In 1949 Senator Cain had again made some headlines with Chaplin—baiting, urging his deportation. In California certain Republican senators were so impressed by the publicity that the House Un-American Activities committee secured in Washington that they began their own hunt for 'subversives' who were trying to destroy the California state constitution. They decided that Chaplin was a subversive character.

The re-issue of *City Lights* in 1950 had been comforting, assuring Chaplin that he did have a market among the people. But the Chaplin-haters were simply lying low for the time. In 1951 and 1952 there were small eruptions of the residual anger of the right wing. They might have been larger, but there was nothing the political and moral absolutists could seize upon. Chaplin was quiet, he had no film out to attack, his personal life was unexceptionable, and he was able to strike back. When the National Broadcasting Company implied he was a communist, he sued for libel.

Here in the autumn of 1952 he was vulnerable again. Chaplin's enemies did not wait long. The *Queen Elizabeth* had scarcely reached mid-Atlantic when Attorney General McGranery announced that the Department of Justice was going to investigate Chaplin. In the Press and in Congress it had been charged that Chaplin was subversive—undermining the government of the United States. Mr McGranery would see whether or not Chaplin should be allowed to return to America.

The crossing was ruined. All the way to Cherbourg Chaplin was worried—but not as his enemies might have hoped, about re-entry. At this point, after years of harassment, he did not care whether he went back to America or not. But his fortune was in America, and this was his concern. He worried lest the United States government find a way to seize his assets.

At Cherbourg the Press was waiting. This time, for a change, Chaplin found the reporters friendly. It was seven years since the end of World War II and for seven years Western Europe had been beholden to the United States, not a very pleasing way of life. In France, particularly, the harassment of Charlot was regarded as an outrage, and the new gesture must also have appealed to latent anti-Americanism. Chaplin suddenly discovered that he had allies and a more than friendly reception.

The same was generally true when they reached London on 24 September. They moved to the Savoy Hotel, and Chaplin began to make plans for the promotion of *Limelight* in Europe.

Very soon the Chaplins decided that Oona must fly back to Los Angeles and remove the securities from the safe deposit box. The poisonous air of America, and the sudden reversal of American policy had left Chaplin shattered. The immigration agent in Los Angeles had been polite and friendly; the moment they left the country they saw the other face of immigration and the shabby political gesture of the government. Chaplin had no further reason to trust anything American. So Oona did return, and took an estimated four-million-dollars-worth of valuables from the safe deposit box. There was still the United Artists Corporation to be broken up and settled, there was still the studio at La Brea and Sunset, there was still the house in Beverly Hills and there were other non-liquid assets. But after Oona came back to London, Chaplin could breathe a sigh of relief. At least he had escaped with dignity.

In America, *Limelight* was greeted tepidly. *Time* magazine did not like it, and many newspapers did not like it either. Some criticized the film on artistic grounds—usually retreating to the ancient complaint that 'the old Charlie' was not there any more. How they would have liked 'the old Charlie' slapstick, silent, and simple in the complex world of 1952 was another matter, one not discussed. William Barrett in the American *Mercury* said he was puzzled why Chaplin should do a film about a failure. Eric Bentley in the *New Republic* called it "a glorious failure".

But in Europe, and in some American publications, *Limelight* was called a logical extension of Chaplin's art and a work of considerable significance on its merits.

Critic Gavin Lambert called it "the elegant melancholy of twilight" borrowing a phrase from Chaplin. "At sixty-three", he said, "Chaplin has executed an imaginative portrait of the artist as an old man and shown his creative powers to be at their height."

J. L. Tallenay, film editor of *La Vie Intellectuel,* offered a French view much in the order of Delluc's discovery early on that Chaplin was the purveyor of sadness. Chaplin, said Tallenay, showed in this film "the deep loneliness and uneasiness of every man who has yielded himself up to the public".

Limelight was a masterpiece, said Tallenay. In America some were calling it a melodrama. It had the melodramatic form, said Tallenay, "but masterpieces are rarely distinguished for the uniqueness of their subject matter or the originality of the form in which they are constructed. The stamp of greatness has to be sought in an author's knowledge of man and in the attitude toward life to which he bears witness."

In the United States and in Europe Charles Chaplin was again much in the news, but on two different planes.

In Washington the Justice Department sententiously announced it was opening investigation into his divorce from Paulette Goddard, seeking information that might indicate "moral turpitude" by Chaplin, which then would enable the Justice Department to deny the re-entry permit. There were a few sober heads in America—*The Nation* represented some of them. Chaplin certainly could not be regarded as a threat to American institutions, said the magazine's editors, and they hoped the administration would retreat from "its ludicrous and humiliating stand".

But to counter sobriety came a new burst of intoxication. Hedda Hopper, the columnist, more or less summed up the views of most of the American Press about Chaplin:

"No one can deny that Chaplin is a good actor. He is. But that doesn't give him the right to go against our customs, to abhor everything we stand for, to throw our hospitality back in our faces. I abhor what he stands for. Good riddance to bad company!"

Even some of the support Chaplin received in America

was left-handed: William Bradford Huie defended Chaplin's right to be obnoxious. Speaking of McGranery and the Justice Department, Huie said: "but if all they can prove is that Chaplin is a stinker, then they are only repeating what has been common knowledge for thirty years, and they should leave the man and his family alone".

By contrast, the reaction in Europe was idyllic.

Graham Greene wrote an open letter to Chaplin, calling him one of the screen's finest artists. The critics of London "choked up" as Mollie Panter-Downes noted, and the concensus had it that *Limelight* was the greatest picture of Chaplin's career. It had, of course, a particularly meaningful viewpoint and milieu for an English audience. But the welcome was genuine and warm, and enhanced greatly by Mr McGranery's outburst of early September.

Chaplin and Oona roamed about London, visiting such old haunts of his as existed, and the people welcomed him gladly. At the Savoy, a secretary was kept busy answering the letters from well-wishers. To be sure it was not like the old days, when it took half a dozen secretaries at the Ritz, but it was a welcome change from the constant flaying he had undergone in America for a decade.

Many letter writers invited him to live with them—in London or Bombay or Milan—and they affirmed their belief in his greatness and reiterated the welcome to his works.

The Chaplins lingered a while in London, sent the children off to a farm for safekeeping, and 'did' the town. They went to Douglas Fairbanks Jr's, for dinner. They visited the Old Vic where Claire Bloom was playing in *Romeo and Juliet.* They attended a concert by Arturo Toscanini. Chaplin did a special broadcast for the BBC on his old films. They went to the première of *Limelight,* and it was just like the old days, cheers and applause and a happy evening. They were presented to royalty, they were given dinners and teas and luncheons.

In Paris in November, Chaplin was greeted as a conquering hero returning home at last. He held a Press conference at the Hôtel Ritz, and the premises were mobbed by friendly journalists, asking friendly questions. The newspapers and magazines treated him as the artist and as the political martyr to American imperialism, or worse, some called it a new fascism.

Limelight opened in the four biggest motion picture houses in Paris, and the lines streamed down the street from morning to night. Paris had always loved Charlot, the French were first to discover that he was more than the slapstick clown, and now they wanted him to stay among them. President Vincent Auriol invited them to the Elysée Palace for lunch. The French government made him an officer of the Legion of Honour, the French intellectuals elected him to the Société des Auteurs et Compositeurs Dramatiques. They were entertained by many people; only the American community showed boorishness. Years earlier Ambassador Myron Herrick in Paris had honoured Chaplin like a hero; now the Americans treated him as a traitor.

Chaplin went on to Rome—again he was fêted heroically, with the small exception of a vegetable attack by young neofascists. He came back to London, where he was invited to Buckingham Palace. Soon he was nominated for the Nobel Peace Prize. One could say that this reception in Europe was overwhelming in the same degree that his departure from America was devastating. The praise came from everywhere, on both sides of the Iron Curtain, and even discounting the propaganda value of a Chaplin dishonoured by America to the Russians, the effect was impressive. A few years later American critic Robert Hatch was to write: "The persecution of Chaplin in the name of American patriotism and public decency is a scandal this era is saddled with forever."

In America the issue continued to sizzle and the Press kept it alive. It was only a part of a major hysterical reaction which Karel Reisz traced in an article in *Sight and Sound* that dealt with the spate of anti-Soviet and anti-communist films that were flooding out of Hollywood.

The Chaplins were faced with a decision as 1953 began. From Washington came the word that the ban on Chaplin's re-entry was still in effect after the new Eisenhower administration came into office. It was to be expected, anti-communism was a major Republican party plank and if they had accused the Democrats of being soft on communism, then, of course, Chaplin would be *persona non grata* because he had been called sympathetic to communism. Dozens of Chaplin's acquaintances were driven from Hollywood and from America for political views they might have held twenty years earlier, or might never have held at all. Chaplin was a lucky man to have enough money so that he did not have to worry about employment.

The Chaplins were torn between remaining in London and moving to Switzerland to live, and in January they visited Switzerland, and began the search for a house. That year Chaplin more or less commuted between London and Lausanne's Beau Rivage Hotel, involved in revivals of old films and the management of his affairs. In April, Chaplin made the final difficult decision, after months of moderate responses to the attacks on him. He delivered his re-entry permit to the American authorities.

"It is not easy to uproot myself and my family from a country where I have lived for forty years without a feeling of sadness," he said. "But since the end of the last World War, I have been the object of lies and vicious propaganda by powerful reactionary groups who by their influence and the aid of America's yellow Press have created an unhealthy atmosphere in which liberal minded individuals can be singled out and persecuted.

"Under these conditions I find it virtually impossible to continue my motion-picture work and I have therefore given up my residence in the United States. . . ."

So the die was cast. It would be pleasant to note that the American press and public reacted in *volte face* to the Chaplin announcement. Unfortunately not, most of those who had qualms about the unrestrained ferocity of the anti-communist movement were lying quiet for self-protection. Good riddance, was the general American attitude toward Chaplin, and it would be a decade before the forces of reason would truly moderate that position.

Chaplin went about his affairs. He bought the £90,000 Manoir de Ban in the village of Corsier near Vevey. He hired a business manager and a secretary. And he moved in to live the life of a country squire. Four more children would be born to the Chaplins here.

In 1953 *Limelight* was doing so badly in America that its continued exhibition had to be reconsidered. When the American Legion threatened to picket the film, it was withdrawn from further circulation in the United States.

Life then settled down for the Chaplins, although there were still problems in America. The Internal Revenue Service claimed that he owed half a million dollars in back taxes, and when he refused to pay it, they imposed penalties that brought the total to nearby a million and half dollars.

He was always an irascible man, and he had quarrelled with many old friends in the past. He quarrelled with his neighbours over domestic problems. He quarrelled with his domestic staff and fired several of them, including his first secretary, who said she had to sue for her pay. He quarrelled with his growing children, as the eldest of them went off to boarding schools. In his own slow, serious fashion, he kept searching for a new idea for a motion picture.

Relations with America grew even a little worse. In the spring of 1954 Oona decided to give up her American citizenship and become a British citizen like Chaplin. The action heaped more coals on the anti-Chaplin movement in America. He was awarded a peace prize by the Communist World Peace Council. In the summer when the powers were meeting in Geneva, Chaplin was fêted by the Russians, and entertained by the Chinese premier Chou En-lai. Red China and Chou were still dreadful names to be invoked in America—Chaplin was again castigated.

In 1955 Chaplin finally divested himself of his shares of United Artists' stock. He was already working on *A King In New York*, which he had chosen from among the many ideas available. Before choosing he had considered a number. Once he had wanted to do a film on Napoleon, and this was studied anew. For years he had kept the idea of doing *Substance and Shadow*, a successful play for which he had bought motion-picture rights in the days when Joan Barry was in his life. But the new motion picture came from deep inside Chaplin, and it reflected the hurt and resentment he felt against the United States.

One evening, Chaplin dined at the Hotel of the Three Crowns in the town, and happened to see the guest-book the establishment maintained for the signatures of notable visitors. Among them were many royal exiles who had come to Switzerland for refuge. An idea was born. King Igor Shadhov of Estrovia, would go to America, the 'land of the free' seeking refuge from tyranny. What would happen there would be drawn from Chaplin's experience and imagination. In 1957 the script was finished. For the first time, Chaplin would ignore the American market. (At the première it became apparent just why.) The film was made at Shepperton and the Chaplins took hotel space at the Great Fosters Hotel at Egham, during the actual filming. Again Chaplin directed and produced, and took the lead. He wrote the story and the screenplay and wrote the music for the film. For his leading lady this time, he chose Dawn Addams, an attractive young English actress who would have basically the same relationship to the film that his leading ladies had in the past. Chaplin films were Chaplin films, and the women's rôle in them was always foreshortened.

King Shadhov came to New York, seeking freedom and beauty as well as sanctuary. Instead, he found commercialism and confusion. He walked through the streets and he went to the pictures, he became involved with the girl, he became involved with American television, and later with the American political system. He had plastic surgery.

In the television sequence one scene reminded of the old Chaplin, when the king choked on the whisky he was supposed to praise.

But the film was Chaplin's answer to anti-Chaplinism, and here it dropped below Chaplin's old level. The boy (played by his son Michael) and his family were involved in attacks by a trouble-hunting American congressional committee. The boy finally testified and 'named names' to save himself, his family, his teachers. After an hour and forty minutes, of mixing pathos and a little of the old Chaplin slapstick, and political commentary, the king gave up the girl, and left America—which had proved to be anything but the land of sanctuary.

Chaplin had great hopes for the film. Major openings were planned for London, Paris, Rome, and Stockholm. But when the film arrived in the early autumn of 1957, it proved a major disappointment. Critic Penelope Houston perhaps summed it all up in one sentence: "Where *Limelight* seemed like a homecoming, a return to the scenes and places out of which Chaplin's art developed, *A King in New York* has about it the remoteness of exile."

There was too much closeness, too much bitterness, too much personal involvement for Charles Chaplin to manage the possible satire of an hysterical America without exaggeration or missing the point. The major difficulty in the film was that it did not come to grips with the universal truths. For as Chaplin later indicated in a conversation with Mrs Harold Stassen, he did not really believe that America was the America of *A King in New York*. A satire on the anti-communist hysteria would have been one thing, but Chaplin erred in soothing his hurts by attacking target after target. No film could succeed in attacking a whole society, and trying to maintain the old Chaplin mystique. In the effort the mystique was lost.

Despite the estrangement between Chaplin and America, he continued in the American news. In the autumn of 1958 his tax troubles with the Internal Revenue Service came to a head, the government threatened to sue, and the suit was settled, Chaplin paying more than he thought he should and not as much as the government wanted.

That year The *Saturday Evening Post* sent writer James P. O'Donnell to Switzerland to do a long profile study of Chaplin in exile. "Poor Charlie, once the funniest man alive, is now a stuffed shirt who has destroyed the peace of a dreamy little Swiss village", was the headline on the first of the three-part series of articles. The articles were heavily based on interviews with Isobel Deluz, his former secretary, and they delved into the home life of the Chaplin family in extreme detail. Mr O'Donnell was very much concerned with Chaplin the man, and his various quirks and habits. The articles were notable, in spite of bias, for a begrudging admiration of Chaplin, with all his warts. Those warts were thoroughly exposed in books by Charles Chaplin Jr, by Lita Grey Chaplin, and by Michael Chaplin, son of Charles and Oona, who had a difficult time finding his own way until he left home for London. Charles Jr, had much the same difficulty, and was to die under tragic circumstances. Sydney, second son of the Lita Grey-Chaplin marriage, was much better adjusted, and became a friend to the new Chaplin family after he bought part interest in a Paris restaurant.

The glare of publicity was a problem, but living in Switzerland kept it to a minimum, and generally speaking, even the most antagonistic writers found Chaplin a much happier fellow than he had been in the old days before Oona. O'Donnell, for example, declared that Oona was Chaplin's buffer against an unfriendly world, and Michael's book indicated much the same.

The year 1959, Chaplin's seventieth, was a good indication of his life in these modern times. A daughter, Annette, was born to Oona that year. Chaplin played tennis, worked on scripts, answered his fan mail, and dickered with various agents in various countries for revivals of the feature films that he alone controlled. He was talking that year about doing something entirely new, making a science fiction film.

Chaplin at seventy was still the creative artist, still in the limelight, still credited even by his enemies, as the greatest comic genius in the history of motion pictures.

15

Reconciliation

The end of the Eisenhower era in America coincided with a leavening of the American attitude toward communism, and whereas in the 1950s Charles Chaplin's relations with Americans were distinctly chilly, in the next decade they began to soften. The relationship between these matters is unfortunate, but the fact was that until the Americans stopped seeing reds under every bed they could not begin to realize that Charles Chaplin, driven from the United States by hysteria, had neither the qualities nor the affiliations to make him suspect of anything but intellectual anarchism.

The year 1962 was a particularly satisfying one for the Chaplins. Their last child, Christopher, was born that year, and Chaplin was honoured with a degree in letters by Oxford University, along with American diplomat Dean Rusk and British painter Graham Sutherland. That year he was busy writing his autobiography, too, a task that gave him much trouble and much pleasure.

Writer Harold Clurman visited Chaplin at Manoir de Ban on behalf of *Esquire*. The article that followed was the most sympathetic treatment of Charles Chaplin that a major American publication had given him in many years. The *Saturday Evening Post* series a few years earlier had painted Chaplin as a crotchety, twisted, unhappy man who quarrelled with everyone around him. It was not that Chaplin who entertained Harold Clurman.

The writer O'Donnell had summarized a possible series of one-reel films based on the Chaplin life, as he discovered it in research that did not seem to include a visit to Chaplin.

"Charlie Buys a Villa ... Charlie Loses the Script in an Airplane ... Oona's Soufflé collapses as Charlie Accepts

World Peace Prize ... Charlie Entertains the Queen of Spain ... The Geneva Conference of Charlie and Chou En-lai ... The London Conference of Charlie and Khruschev ... Charles Shows the Swiss How to Build a Tennis Court ... Charlie Gets the Legion of Honour (French release) ... Charlie Received at St James's Palace by the Captain of the Queen's Guards (British release) ... Charles Shows the Swiss How to Build a swimming Pool."

Clurman told how he was met at Lausanne Station by Chaplin in his chauffeured Bentley and they then drove the thirty minutes to Vevey, stopping at a school in Lausanne to pick up the three youngest children. Unlike the four eldest, the young ones were growing up as Europeans; Clurman had the impression that French was more natural to them than English as a basic language, although the Chaplins kept an English governess among the seventeen servants, one of whose basic functions was to keep them speaking English. This little problem told a great deal about the change; ten years had passed since the quarrel with the United States government and the Chaplins' links with the past were growing weak. As the animosity of America dimmed towards Chaplin, so did his own resentment dim.

Clurman found Oona relaxed and beautiful, as marvellous a hostess as ever. They drank martinis on the terrace overlooking Lake Geneva. They dined and talked of old friends in America, and Chaplin found he was forgetting some of the names. That night Clurman read some of the autobiography. He was pleasantly surprised by the even tenor of it. Chaplin had told him that he, himself, was surprised at how well America had come off in the book. It was true.

"For the first time in my long acquaintance with Chaplin," wrote Clurman, "I had the feeling that he was not only an artist of genius but a man who might be considered—or who had become—wise."

And their conversation in this visit indicated the mellowing of a generous nature.

"I can't stand Communists with their *system* .... I hate systems .... " Chaplin said at one point. How sad that it came so late, for that little admission, made a dozen years ago, would have saved Chaplin untold months of agony, and might have saved an American government from making a whole nation look foolish.

Chaplin was effusive and joyous on this visit. He spoke of his art, and his love for Oona, and his happiness in the life they had made for themselves. When Clurman asked if he would like to return to America, he tactfully avoided the question. "I am very happy here", was the answer, and Clurman equally tactfully left it at that.

For a moment at least, Chaplin had touched on American territory a few months earlier. They were making a trip around the world by air with the older children, a holiday primarily, prompted by Chaplin's desire to see again those far places where he had been welcomed so heartily. The trip was notable for one aspect that indicated the happy change in Chaplin's affairs since his move to Europe: the Western Press paid virtually no attention to him.

Chaplin's brief encounter with America came at Anchorage, Alaska, where the plane landed to refuel. Only when he had stepped on Alaskan soil did Chaplin remember that Alaska was now the 49th American state. He scurried back into the aircraft, and sat there for two hours, worrying lest the American immigration officers arrest him, take away his papers, and throw him into jail. The scars of the past were obviously very deep, and even the friendly attitude of the officers on duty did not completely reassure him.

They went to Japan and were met by a cheering crowd, then escorted into Tokyo with a motorcade of police, to another reception at the hotel entrance. It was like the old days. The whole stay was like that. On to Hong Kong, more receptions, and the same at Singapore.

So the children grew. Geraldine and Michael left home not many years later, Geraldine to study at the Royal Ballet School; Michael to wrench himself from security and join for a time the hippy cult of London.

In 1964 came a revival of old Chaplin films in London. But of course they had scarcely ever been missing from one cinema or another, and even in 1976 strollers in Piccadilly raising their eyes to the marquees would see one bearing the unmistakeable figure of the little fellow. That year, 1964, also marked the publication of the autobiography, which was generally greeted as 'not enough'. Chaplin had chosen to deal with his life and friends, not with his films. He left the American lady author ungratified—he did not 'tell all' about the loves of his youth; to a man as shy and sensitive as Chaplin he told a great deal, considering the fact that Oona was very much by his side.

In 1966, Chaplin made his next film, *The Countess from Hong Kong*. Earlier he had told the writer Margaret Hinxman that when he saw Marlon Brando in *The Men* he had felt that he would like some day to use Brando in a film of his own. *The Countess from Hong Kong* was the result. It was in many ways the most pretentious film Chaplin had made, and although he wrote the story and the screenplay and directed the film himself, he played only a walk-on rôle as an old porter. This picture really had very little of the old Chaplin in it.

Life in Vevey went on in its slow and comfortable way. In 1969 almost on his eightieth birthday, Chaplin was nominated for the Nobel Prize for literature, and later in the year he was back in London, seeing old friends. He gave a literary luncheon to honour Noel Coward. He saw Douglas Fairbanks Jr, and Pablo Casals and J. B. Priestley. He considered making other films, but decided against it for the time. He was interviewed and he broadcast and he even appeared on television in London.

In 1972 Chaplin returned to the United States for his first visit in many years. Most of his old enemies were dead and gone, and even the yellow Press had become decidedly more restrained and liberal than ever before. There was no Westbrook Pegler to insult him, no William Randolph Hearst to turn demons against him, no Hedda Hopper to consign him to purgatory. The Statue of Liberty was there, the tall building still stood, but the America of 1972 was not the land that had ejected the comic genius so despicably exactly twenty years before. Chaplin went back to Hollywood on this visit, to find most of the old studios torn down and the place changed so completely he could hardly recognize it. The trip was a triumph in every way, he was welcomed and loved and given an Oscar by the Academy of Theatre Arts.

Many friends and old acquaintances asked Chaplin if he would not come back to the United States to live. He smiled and was polite, but indicated how happy he and the family were in Vevey. And it was true; twenty years had gone by and the Chaplins had, as a family, become Europeans. True, Charles never acquired more than passing familiarity with the French language, but Oona was competent to deal with the daily problems, and Chaplin surrounded himself with English speakers to meet his intellectual and professional needs.

For years after leaving Hollywood, Chaplin had toyed with various ideas for films. He planned a motion picture called *The Freak,* based on the tragedy of the dreadfully warped person he had seen in the household when he was on tour of the British provinces with Karno's troupe. But in 1970 he postponed it, and postponed it once again. There were so many other things to do.

Business affairs occupied much of Chaplin's working time. New generations had come along to hear of Charles Chaplin and Charlot, and they wanted to see his films. *The Circus,* for example, had never been seen in Britain before the 1970s. Then it was taken out of mothballs and opened in London. *Limelight* became acceptable in America after the celebrated reunion of 1972, and the film was shown around the country. That same year *Modern Times* was revived in London, and reviewed with the excitement and attention given many another new film.

The revivals continued. Russia staged a festival of Chaplin films. So did France in 1974. In England, Chaplin was often called upon for broadcasts on the BBC on the film arts, or on his own work, and when the television people could capture him on his frequent visits to London, he was interviewed and examined. In this period of his life, Chaplin had grown far more receptive to the Press and to interviewers generally, possibly because there were not so many of them, and they did not harry him as they had once. Long forgotten by the new generations were the scrappy encounters of the 1920s, 1930s, and the dismal ones of the 1940s and 1950s.

Chaplin's birthdays were celebrated widely in the world. *The Times* never failed to take note of them, nor did the Paris newspapers. The Soviets acclaimed him too, and did him the signal honour of publishing his autobiography in Moscow. It was one of the few life stories of a modern Westerner ever printed there.

Chaplin gathered his family around him. The relations with the two elder sons were as good as they might be until Charles Jr's tragic death in 1968. Sydney and the Chaplins always got on famously, and that liking and respect was transferred to the children in a way quite unusual among layered families.

Life at the Manoir de Ban was very pleasant, 'greased' for Charles Chaplin, as it were, by the never-ending efforts of Oona to seek his comfort and satisfaction. Even in the worst days, when the American Press could find nothing right with Chaplin, the detractors could find nothing wrong with Oona.

Chaplin was not an easy father. Geraldine, the eldest of the children, got on well enough until she went to London to make her own career. Then she had her ups and downs, duly chronicled in the Press, but maintained a reasonable relationship with the family.

Michael Chaplin had a more difficult time of it. He was a small boy when the Chaplins moved to Europe, and the transition was not easy for him. At first the Chaplins all lived at the Savoy, then the children were literally 'farmed out' to a working establishment in Berkshire. They lived at the Hotel Beau Rivage near Lausanne until the Manoir de Ban was ready, and then the hiatus was over—the Chaplins settled down to the new life.

Again it was hard for the older children. They were cast into a French-speaking school at Corsier, and had to sink or swim. They swam, with varying degrees of success, Michael perhaps achieving the least. He was dispatched to a private school in Montreux, but proved too much for the school to handle, and was sent to board at the Ecole Nouvelle de Paudex. He resisted education; even two cram-courses at the St Bernard monks' school did not arouse his interest in matters academic. He was much more successful with the guitar. As for the future, Michael decided he wanted to be an actor. As noted, he had parts in two of the Chaplin films in these years. That degree of accomplishment and independence encouraged him, and shortly after the Chaplins returned from their world tour in 1961, Michael decided to break away from the home ties.

As a teenager, Michael became involved with girls, and then with the police, in a manner that Charles did not like. Michael was picked up by a detective in Lausanne and sent home on the train. Chaplin had learned the facts of his son's indiscretions, and was furious. Here is how Michael later recalled it in his book *I Couldn't Smoke the Grass on My Father's Lawn,* as Michael came home to the Manoir de Ban and found his father waiting for him on the hall stairway:

The moment I walked in he leaped down the steps and with a sudden movement, slapped my face hard with the back of his hand. He must have been waiting there for hours, the whole business in the past few months boiling up inside him. . . . I ran up the steps and paused in one corner of the hallway. My father stood at the other end glaring up at me, his fist tightly clenched.
"You poor young fool," he shouted, "letting yourself be swept off your feet by a woman of twice your years. Why didn't you leave her alone when I told you to months ago?"
I turned away, unable to speak, and sensed my mother's presence halfway up the stairs.
"What have you done to the boy?" she asked quietly.
"I hope I have spanked him hard enough to teach him to do as he is told", he replied sharply, as he climbed past her up the stairs to his bedroom. I heard the door slam behind him and then there was silence.
My mother came over to me.
"Poor boy", she said softly, "poor silly boy. What an idiot you are. . . . "

As a result of that escapade, Michael Chaplin was sent to the International School at Geneva as a boarder. Almost immediately he was again in trouble with girls and the school authorities. When Geraldine was in London in the early 1960s, attending the Royal Ballet School, Michael visited her several times, and finally ran away from school to London. He refused to return, promised that he would find a school in London and study for his 'O' levels, and that was the best the Chaplins could do with him.

So Michael Chaplin became a Londoner but one of the drugged generation. He did go to school, but so seldom that at examination time he did not even sit for the exams. He had a job with designer Adam Polloc for a few months. Of course he was a spoiled boy. He travelled in exclusive company. But soon enough Chaplin lowered his sights; he became a confirmed smoker of marijuana and so far refused to meet parental wishes that Chaplin cut off his allowance. For the next few years, he was in and out of scrapes with the police and other authorities, travelling with young men and women of like mind to the Riviera, to Spain, to Italy—anywhere for amusement and new thrills. He paired with an aspiring actress name Patrice Johns. Michael wanted to marry Patrice, but Chaplin objected since he was under age. Yet he was old enough in 1964 to marry in Scotland, and then to go without a job, to live in a flat in Belsize Park, Hampstead, and to apply for National Assistance. That caused the final break with the family.

Michael continued in the news from time to time, and so did Geraldine, and any other Chaplin who managed to push his or head above the crowd. The Chaplins were news, in the 1960s and the 1970s as they had always been. But those were the new generations of Chaplins, trying to live their own lives in their own ways.

As for Charles and Oona Chaplin, the pace slowed in the 1970s, after the ultimate victory of the triumphal American tour. A new generation of publicists had arisen too, one unhampered by the grim memories of past quarrels between Chaplin and the Press. What little news came out of Vevey was usually positive, but it was less and less each year. Chaplin tended his correspondence and considered projects. He fended off ridiculous suggestions, such as promoters who attempted to use his name to further the sale of a rejuvenating substance. He guarded his films, their rights, and his own good name against scandalmongers—as in the past.

But mostly, as Chaplin had for the past twenty years, he enjoyed the life of the Manoir de Ban. In his eighties, uninhibited by some of the shynesses of the past, he

frequently remarked on his love for Oona, the woman who
had been the perfect wife to him.

There was talk about a knighthood for Charles Chaplin
and had been for a number of years. In England, as in
America, the rigours of the past were forgotten in the 1970s.
And in the Honours list of 1975, the knighthood came. It was
the last great gesture of acclaim for the little man who had
done so much to make the world a better place, whose films
reminded and would continue to remind the people of the
world that happiness and tragedy are the lot of humanity,
but that always as with the little fellow, there is a horizon
ahead, and over that horizon lies hope.

Bibliography

Bowman, William D., *Charlie Chaplin, his life and art* (Routledge & Kegan Paul, 1931).

Chaplin, Charles, *My Autobiography* (Bodley Head, 1964).

——, *My Wonderful Visit* (Hurst & Blackett, 1922).

——, *My Life in Pictures* (Bodley Head, 1974).

Chaplin, Charles Jr, *My Father* (Longmans, Green, 1960).

Chaplin, Lita Grey, *My Life With Chaplin, an intimate memoir* (B. Geiss Assoc., 1966).

Chaplin Michael, *I Couldn't Smoke the Grass on My Father's Lawn* (Leslie Frewin, 1966).

Codd, Elsie, *Charles Chaplin's Methods* (1920).

Cotes, Peter and Niklaus T., *The Little Fellow* (Paul Elek, 1952).

Dell, Draycot, *The Charlie Chaplin Scream Book* (The Fleetway House, 1915).

Delluc, L., *Charlie Chaplin* (Lane, 1922).

Forsell, Lars, *Chaplin* (Stockholm: Wahlström & Widshand, 1953).

Gifford, Denis, *Chaplin* (Macmillan, 1974).

Huff, Theodore, *Charlie Chaplin* (Cassells, 1952).

Leprohon, Pierre, *Charles Chaplin* (Paris: J. Melot, 1946).

McCaffrey, Donald, *Focus on Chaplin* (Prentice Hall, 1971).

——, *Four Great Comedians* (Zwemmer, 1968).

Manvell, Roger, *Chaplin,* 1974.

Minney, Rubeigh, *Chaplin the Immortal Tramp* (Newnes, 1954).

Payne, Robert, *The Great Charlie* (André Deutsch, 1957).

——, *The Great God Pan* (Hermitage House, 1952).

Pina, Francisco, *Charles Chaplin* (1952).

Poulaille, Henry, *Charles Chaplin* (1927).

Quigly, Isabel, *Charlie Chaplin, early comedies* (Studio Vista, 1968).

198   *Sir Charlie*

Reed, Langford, *The Chronicles of Charles Chaplin* (Cassell, 1917).

Von Ulm, Gerith, *Charlie Chaplin, King of Tragedy* (Caxton Printers, 1940).

Cinema: Practical Course in Cinema Acting (National Business and Personal Efficiency Department of Standards, Art Book Co. Ltd, London).

The following magazines and newspapers were also consulted:

Sight and Sound, Cambridge Journal, World Review, Sequence 7, Sewanee Review, London Mercury, New Statesman, Sunday Times, Times Literary Supplement, Illustrated London News, Nation, Harper's, New Republic, Cinema Studies, Guardian, Partisan Review, Spectator, Saturday Evening Post, Saturday Review, Reporter, Coronet, New York Times Magazine, Esquire, American Mercury, New Yorker, Theatre Arts, Commonweal.

Index

Chaplin, Annette, 186

——, Charles: becomes celebrity, 67-9; birth, 24; character, personal, 18, 21, 24-6, 29, 32, 37, 40, 49, 64-5, 73, 80, 99-105, 110-11, 117-19, 121, 132, 135, 143, 159, 162, 166, 169-70, 183, 185, 189, 194; childhood, 17-9; critics of, 14-5, 19, 76-7, 79-81, 83, 117-19, 121, 152-53, 159, 162-63, 166-70, 176-80, 182-83, 185, 187; divorces, 13, 108-10, 117-18, 159-60, 179; early career, 22-41; education, 22-3, 28-9, 37, 41, 43, 47, 99, 119, 144; 'era' ended, 154-58; finances, 22, 64, 67-8, 71, 88-9, 103-4, 112, 117-18, 127, 142, 154, 159, 162, 175, 177-78, 183, 185; gives up U.S. residence, 182; homes, 10, 17, 21, 25-6, 28, 76, 96, 106, 116, 154, 171, 182, 188, 192; honours, 16, 101, 145, 181, 183, 187, 190-91, 195; knighted, 16, 195; marriages, 21, 82-3, 88, 90, 106-9, 115-19, 124, 138, 154, 161, 171, 189; 'method' the, 128-32; politics, 16-19, 23, 92-4, 97, 99, 101, 103, 144, 147-51, 153-54, 158-59, 162, 166-70, 182, 187-88; Press, relations with, 14, 91-4, 98, 105, 107-12, 115-17, 137, 143-45, 154, 158-59, 161-62, 167, 169, 175-80, 182, 185-86, 189-92, 194; re-entry ban, 181; religion, 26; scandals, 13, 107-9, 117-18, 121, 137, 161, 166; trip abroad, 93-102; visit to the U.S., 191-92, 194;

world tour, 143-45; youth, 24-35.

——, Charles, Jr., 173-74, 185-86, 192

——, Charles Spencer, 24, 26-30, 104

——, Christopher, 187

——, Geraldine, 171, 174, 189, 192-94

——, Hannah, 24-9, 31, 35-7, 46, 104, 110, 131-32

——, Josephine, 171, 174

——, Lita Grey, 21, 114-18, 121, 138, 152, 173, 185-86

——, Michael, 171, 174, 184-86, 189, 192-94

——, Mildred Harris, 21, 82, 106-9

——, Oona O'Neill, 14, 161-62, 171, 175-76, 178, 180, 183, 185-92, 194-95

——, Sidney, 24, 27, 30-6, 43, 46, 56, 64, 67, 69-70, 104, 110, 145

——, Sydney Earle, 117, 174, 186, 192

——, Victoria, 171

Charlot, see Tramp, the

Chase, Charley, 61

Chase Me Charlie, 71

Cherrill, Virginia, 138-39

Chicago, 65, 69

Chou En-lai, 183

Churchill, Sir Winston, 13, 16, 144

Ciné Pour Tous, Le, 128

Circus, The, 135-38, 191

City Lights, 11, 33, 59, 138-42, 169, 177

Clifton, Emma, 55

Clurman, Harold, 20, 187-89

Codd, Elsie, 128, 130

Collier, Constance, 173